FIFTY SHADES OF ABUSE

BY

#ONEVOICE

The home for victims & survivors

TEXT COPYRIGHT © 2013 EVE THOMAS/#ONEVOICE

ALL RIGHTS RESERVED

No part of this book may be reproduced, stored in a retrieval system or transmitted in any form or by any means without the prior written permission of the publisher, Eve Thomas, except by a reviewer who may quote brief passages in a review to be printed in a newspaper, magazine or journal.

Second printing

All the chapters contained within this book are factual accounts of domestic violence/abuse. Each one has been written by a victim/survivor of the global problem that is DOMESTIC VIOLENCE.

All profit is to be donated to charities that work tirelessly in helping victims/survivors around the world.

The stories you read from both victims and survivors have not been edited in anyway. Each chapter is their voice, their words written straight from the heart.

Please read with caution. These stories are often graphic in nature.

MESSAGE

When a team walks off the field victorious over a formidable foe each team member themselves have overcome a personal battle that together made the team stronger. These individual stories of overcoming ones foes, together, unite us all and hopefully provide inspiration and strength to others as well. As a choir is filled with many individual voices, when in harmony, one voice of triumph fills the air.

R. Dana Browne

R. Dana Browne is a former Police Detective now an actor based in Los Angeles.

INTRODUCTION

To All Who Read This Book

My name is Chris Flux and I'm the Campaign Director for an organisation called **Men Against Violence** which is based in Preston, Lancashire in the UK. We are a *"men's campaign to end violence against women"* by engaging men (and women) with issues such as domestic abuse, sexual violence and exploitation. We are doing this through education, awareness raising and encouraging people to speak out against abuse.

I first came across Eve Thomas on Twitter in February 2013 and we took much interest in each other's work. She has written two novels giving a real insight into the issue of domestic abuse and violence. They may be fiction but as a survivor herself the books accurately reflect the reality of life within an abusive relationship. As someone dedicated to ending domestic abuse along with other forms of violence it is a great privilege to introduce this book.

I must admit I am not a survivor myself and was lucky to grow up in a house with two parents who respected each other. Yet this does not mean I am unaffected by the injustice of domestic abuse. It's an issue that has always angered me! Close friends of mine have been abused and as someone who was bullied at school I have some understanding of what it's like to be victimised. However I'm sure that whilst you will find the stories in this book to be (at times) difficult to read, you will also find their stories of courage and recovery to be truly inspiring! Survivors of abuse are often seen by society as weak and helpless 'victims' to be pitied. Yet all of the people contributing to this book, whilst at times experiencing vulnerability, have somehow found the amazing strength to not only go from being a *victim* to a *survivor*, but to take action by sharing their story with the world.

And now I would like to SPEAK TO THE MEN (mostly): Despite the stereotype of men as 'violent apes', the majority of men are not abusers. Abusive behaviour is not some natural innate male (or female) characteristic. It's a deliberate choice, not an inevitability overspill of male energy. However male violence is a common problem in our society and whilst there is some incredible work done by women, it's only going to end completely when we guys decide to end it both collectively and individually.

IF YOU HAVE BEEN ABUSIVE: You **can** change! Violence is a choice, so non-violence can also be chosen. But the change has to be genuine and permanent, not a temporary thing.

It's no use blaming it on alcohol, stress, your upbringing or provocation. Many people face all of these things and yet do not abuse. It's no use an abuser saying that they "lost it" either, because most abusers don't attack their boss at work even when under great stress because they know there are serious consequences for doing so. You must do the hard work of accepting full responsibility for your behaviour and refuse to blame anyone else. However change is definitely possible and there is professional help available to support you to do this. A good first step is to remove yourself from the home where the abuse is happening (if possible) and not return until you have completely changed.

FOR THE GOOD MEN: We have an important role in ending the violence in society. We can (directly and indirectly) challenge the abusive behaviour and sexist attitudes of others. We can learn about the issues, educate others, be a supportive friend to survivors and be a positive male role model to the men and boys around us. Each of us has different skills and a different sphere in society that we can influence. For example a businessman raise funds for a refuge and a sports coach can lead by example when working with young men. That is the whole purpose of the **Men Against Violence** campaign as well as other groups like our partners the **White Ribbon Campaign**.

Finally, TO SURVIVORS: We are completely on your side and many good men are working hard alongside women to prevent further abuse and ensure that you get the justice that you deserve!

In Solidarity,

Mr Chris Flux

(Campaign Director)

Website and Social Media Links

Website: www.menagainstviolence.co.uk
Facebook: Men Against Violence (Preston)
Twitter: @MAV_Preston
White Ribbon Campaign UK: www.whiteribboncampaign.org.uk

CHAPTER ONE

My name is Heather but I am really known by my pen name, the name that was created in memory of my grandparents, Eve Thomas. I am the author of The Eyes and Choices-The Darker Years, a passionate campaigner, a Tiny Peacefighter and above all else a mum. I was also a victim of domestic violence/abuse for over twenty one years; I say was because the title I wear with the most pride is SURVIVOR!

For a very long time I didn't recognise what was happening to me how my life gradually slipped away until I was trapped with no one and nowhere to turn. I no longer recognised the truth, my life a constant web of lets downs and lies. I lived for the good days, the smiles and laughter but as the years passed by they happened less and less.

This is my story, the words not those of an author but a survivor, a mum and so straight from the heart. Forgive me if I ramble but I like the other 49 voices in this book have found my voice, a voice that I dream will be heard around the world. Now I was a little firework back in the day but slowly my sparkle disappeared as I became a totally different person, my old self lost as gradually I submitted to my abusers demands. The constant verbal put downs were the worst and his words left deep scars that I still fight every single day to overcome. Bruises, cuts and broken bones hurt like hell and there have been many times that I genuinely feared for my life but for me the emotional abuse was the worst and "his" words will haunt me forever no matter how hard I try to fight them.

I use the word fight because I am no longer a victim, I broke free and I've worked hard to become the survivor I am today. There is life after domestic violence, THERE IS HOPE. I guess I will always shudder when I hear the word "ugly" and the amount of times I heard "I'm too good for you, bet you thought you'd won the lottery" are countless but I am trying. I spent many years thinking I was never good enough but guess what, I AM GOOD ENOUGH! I have mountains to climb where self confidence is concerned but I am getting there, I am a survivor! When I look in the mirror now I see a different woman looking back at me, a happier more carefree female who welcomes each day with a smile.

I refuse to allow his words to cause me any further pain, HE WILL NOT WIN! HE WILL NOT BREAK ME!

Once, in my past life, I was almost broken. He'd threatened over the years, usually whilst grasping a handful of my hair that he would "Break me." He almost did. My mind was not my own, I began to doubt my own thoughts and actions and he nearly drove me crazy but I had my saviour, my courageous leading lady and so I poured every feeling and emotion I experienced into her story.

I couldn't reach out, I was petrified and so I secretly buried myself in my writing and from my anguish Amy was born, through her I could unburden my pain and I kind of reached out to her for help. The life I created for her made mine seem like a dream as I poured out my misery with every word I typed; if her world, her life was a disaster then mine seemed normal. It was through Amy that I found the courage to seek help and so her ending was re-written as I took the journey myself and discovered the cocoon of help and safety that arrived from the moment I walked into the police station.

My abuser tried over the years to stop me from writing but I had a secret, Amy and I was determined he wouldn't find her, she was special she was going to help me one day to realise my dream to help others and so I made sure I covered my tracks with short stories, many of which he either deleted or burnt and a creative writing course with the Open University but he never found her, never found my secret hiding place where I stowed my memory stick.

Writing helped me so much and with this in mind I wanted to reach out to others and offer them the opportunity to share their pain so that they could hopefully progress even further on their journey of being a survivor. Many have told me that as they have typed out their own personal stories it has helped them to heal, all I can say is I'm happy I could share this with you all. I've managed to give fifty survivors a voice, a voice that will NOT be silenced and I hope there will be many more. One in four women are affected by domestic violence in the UK, 2 women die every week, hundreds and thousands of children are living their childhoods surrounded by abuse – WHEN WILL IT STOP? WHEN WILL THE ABUSERS STOP? Do you know that more women are injured because of domestic violence than cancer and that domestic violence costs my country alone £16 billion, yes £16 billion a year?! Shocking but true facts.

The history around the creation of this book began on twitter and I am truly amazed at how wonderful you all are. I hope that this collection of stories raises not only awareness but oodles of money for something that is very close to my heart. What began as an angry rant at EL James, the author of the Fifty Shades of Grey trilogy after she made hurtful comments which insulted and offended victims and survivors everywhere has now become a vehicle to highlight domestic violence/abuse; a tool that I can only hope puts DV firmly in the spotlight!

I sincerely hope that E L James reads this book, maybe then she will be able to see the domestic abuse that is so clearly evident in her books, maybe then she will apologise for her cruel and abusive words.

My personal message to E L James that I originally posted on my website blog to warn Ms James about the publication of this book.

Dear Ms James

I mean you no harm by publishing this book and I personally would like to reach out to you and offer the hand of peace.

We are both authors, the conductors of our words and with this in mind I ask you to take ownership of your words, words that have injured millions of women, men and children.

I congratulate you on your success and hope one day we can meet so I may speak with you on a personal level and explain just why your words both offended and hurt me.

I hope you will take the time to read this book, a collection of factual stories all with a common theme that I hope you will one day empathise with. Domestic violence/abuse is a global problem, one that is clearly evident as we go about our day to day lives. I do not live in a bubble Ms James, I live in the real world and you used to too before Grey brought you fame. I feel it is very sad that you have lost yourself Ms James.

I apologise in advance for the lead story and from one woman to another I can only pray, as does the author, that you will see that Fifty Shades Of Grey is abuse not romance and has in fact destroyed this young woman's life.

Kindest regards

Eve x

Women throughout the world have taken Christian Grey into their hearts, these women are unable to see the abuse and even though the original mission of this book has changed I still hope that these women see that the character that E L James created is an abuser and that Fifty Shades Of Grey is NOT a love story but a tale of domestic violence and abuse. The lead story in this book is horrific and I have promised faithfully to protect the author who wishes to remain anonymous. My lips are sealed but I want to reach out to you – you are a very brave woman to come forward and share your story with me, with the world is something that has required so much courage.

I know that you do so wanting to raise awareness that Fifty Shades Of Grey is abuse but your story highlights so much more. I shall say no more………

I shall end my chapter with a little more about myself. You are probably wondering why I stayed for so long in a relationship that clearly wasn't right, the answer is difficult but I will try to explain a little although I hope you will understand that a lot is very personal to me and there are something's that I will never speak about although I'm becoming braver every day.

When I was 21 years old I met my abuser, a charming man who was 6 years older than me. My parents divorced when I was young and so there was just me, my mum and my sister, no brothers to protect me and keep me safe. My grandma had passed away quite suddenly the year before and my Granddad was very ill and slowly dying of a broken heart.

Looking back I honestly think my abuser recognised this, he saw in me a potential victim.

The first time he hit me he begged for forgiveness and even though it went against everything I had been taught I stayed, I don't know why.......

A few weeks later I took ill in the middle of the night, in agony I was rushed into hospital and straight into theatre. I had a fallopian tube infection and was told I would probably never be able to have children, I was devastated. I remember crying and he held me tight and promised that it didn't matter, it was better just the two of us anyway.

He picked me up a few days later and took me back to his flat but I was a different person, I felt empty. I cried a lot over the next few weeks and regretted ever saying that I wanted a career not kids, now that choice had been taken away from me and I honestly felt as if I was somehow being punished for my words. I was 21, almost 22 years old and I was in a relationship that I knew wasn't right but I couldn't have children, who would want me?

He was quick to use it against me, to hurt me and I can still remember how much it hurt when he told me how useless I was, how I couldn't give him babies.........

I came off the pill, I mean what was the point and I carried on, determined that I wouldn't let it or him beat me and so I put my head down, went back to work and pretended it had all never happened.

A few months later a letter arrived from the hospital, an appointment to see Dr. Falconer. I remember walking into his office and feeling immediately at ease, he had the biggest smile ever and a carnation in the lapel of his jacket. (I now know that Dr Falconer always wore a fresh carnation every day to work.) He asked me some questions and then I lay down on the bed to be examined.

As he prodded and poked my tummy he looked at me funny and pulling at the hem of my top instructed me I could get up.

I was off for a scan and although a little worried I was more concerned with the amount of water they honestly expected me to drink and hold without dashing off to the loo for a pee!

The lady squirted the cold jelly onto my stomach and began to roll the machine over me, I was giggling, it really tickled and as Dr. Falconer walked into the room I tried my best to behave, gosh I was nervous!

NERVOUS! Shit I was pregnant! 12 weeks pregnant! I think within that next ten minutes I felt every single emotion possible and all with a very full bladder!

I don't remember the journey home, I don't remember much of the next few months, I was so happy! The physical abuse tailed off whilst I was pregnant but the verbal was still there only now he thought it was hysterical to laugh at me waddling about, he took great delight in telling me just how ugly I looked whilst I was pregnant and how that after I had the baby, if I could even manage that with being such a poison dwarf, (I'm only 4ft 10") he wouldn't want to come near me, my body was ruined.

Please, don't get me wrong he was nice as well, very protective but the abuse was always there in the background, the threats.

I didn't care, I was pregnant and although I felt very uncomfortable towards the end I did it, I had my baby. Sophie was born and from the moment I held her I was in love, she was perfect, gorgeous, she was my baby. I WAS A MUM! Sophie was such an easy baby and although we had a little scare when she was only a few weeks old she progressed quickly and passed her first hearing test with flying colours.

Life continued, the abuse continued and I continued to plod along hoping that one day he would change, one day he would love his family enough to get help. Sophie was two years old when I found out I was pregnant again! I remember going home after my doctor's appointment with a beaming smile on my face, he was in the bathroom having a shave and I popped my head around the door, Sophie in my arms.

"Hello daddy, I'm pregnant." I announced.

His face said it all but the words that followed I will never forget.

"You better be fucking joking, get rid!"

Sadly I lost my baby a few weeks later but only months later I was pregnant again! Yes I was pregnant for the 3rd time and the hospital said I could probably never have kids! PFT, I had shown them!

Days after finding out I was pregnant my abuser sat on my stomach and punched me in the face, cutting the underneath of my eye. I rang the police but was told to sort my relationship out and I am going to be very honest I was asked what I had done to upset him! I was so upset, I didn't know how to get angry back then and being genuinely afraid for my safety and the safety of my babies I pleaded with the police man to help me.

Reluctantly a statement was taken, he was arrested and we split up.

I was distraught! I knew he was wrong, I knew I was a victim but at 17 weeks pregnant I was rushed into hospital after I started bleeding and going into labour and there I stayed until Katie was born by emergency C section at 31 weeks.

I had no one, he drove me away from my family and so the only person who could look after Sophie was him, I'm ashamed to say I took him back and as I am typing this I am crying at the broken woman I was.

Katie was almost two weeks old when I held her for the first time; my baby was held by everyone else but me....

When I was in the early stages of pregnancy they found that I had placenta praevia this unfortunately turned into placenta accreta and with the full team of doctors in the operating theatre, various different attempts to save my womb and life not to mention 25 units of blood they performed an emergency hysterectomy. I was 25 years old.

I was put on a ventilator whilst my shocked body recovered and when I was re-introduced to the world several days later I was entirely broken.

The first time I visited my daughter in the special care baby unit will be something I will never forget, she was so tiny, her little legs stuck straight up in the air but her eyelashes! Katie had the thickest, blackest, longest eyelashes I had ever seen and a tuft of almost white hair, she was gorgeous!

I was bloody petrified! Feeding her was hard, burping her was traumatic, she was sooooo tiny. When we brought her home I was scared stiff, I was not only responsible for my little Sophie but also Katie whose needs were massive.

Every three hours the alarm would bleep to let me know it was time for another feed to stop hypothermia setting in, I was exhausted and thanked God that Sophie was such an easy little girl, give her a pan and a spoon and she would spend hours banging, give her a toy mind you and she would spend hours trying to pull it apart to see how it worked. Sophie and her love for screwdrivers, plug sockets and anything that could be taken apart is a whole other story, one that kept me on my toes for her entire childhood! ☺

Katie was 8 weeks old when she turned blue in her pram. I had mentioned the bluish/black tinge around her mouth often to the special care midwives, each one telling me that is was wind and very common in premature babies but this was different, her whole face was literally darkening before my eyes. I rang 999 and resuscitated my baby whilst I waited for the ambulance. Lumbar punctures, blood tests, EEG's, ECG's followed and finally Katie was diagnosed with possible Woolfe Parkinson's White Syndrome, a heart defect.

We were sent home with an apnoea monitor and strict instructions and the next few years passed in a whizz of bleeping alarms, very little sleep and many hospital visits, most of which he refused to attend.

The abuse continued both physical and emotional and I was always reminded that I was young, ugly with two children and no womb, "who the fuck would want you." I believed him, I stayed.

As my girls grew the physical stuff became more subtle, the odd dig here, the casual arm around the shoulder, the fingertips that press into your skin just that tad too hard, the tug of your hair as you feel his fingers winding in it behind your back – all little gestures to let you know he was there, listening, watching. I was dead inside.

I tried to be me, I tried to smile and laugh and over the years I became a very good actress learning to adapt to each new situation, never letting anyone close enough to know the real truth.

After the hysterectomy I became very poorly, mentally and even when I recovered from this he used it against me telling me that social services would take my girls away from me because I was mental, crazy in the head.

And so I stayed and as my girls grew they began to make comments, express their concerns and slowly I realised it wasn't me, I was a victim and my husband was nothing more than a violent, verbally abusive bully. I began to write and Amy was born, finally I had someone to talk to, finally I could share my pain. I spent as much time as I could writing, escaping into the world I created and I cannot express how much a fictional character actually helped me, she saved my life!

I made a decision, once Katie was over 16 years of age I could leave because no court, no judge, no social worker would make her have contact with him if she didn't want to and so I lived my life for the next few years, confiding in Amy, seeking guidance from the courageous woman I had created.

I still can't really talk about the end that much but the mind games, the lies almost destroyed me, I was a shell. He had help in the end, another woman who also thought it was good fun to have me think I was going insane. I almost lost my house, I was threatened repeatedly by not only him but her and I ended up a mess but what hurt me the most was the way I almost lost my mind at the hands of my husband, the father of my children and another woman.

I've had many years of hell but 2010 for me was the worse, the man I married, the father of my children used my hysterectomy and subsequent depression to make me think I was ill.

I remember getting in my car and driving to my local hospital, I wanted them to admit me, I needed help. My daughters saved me that day but not before I'd flung a pair of scissors across the kitchen that stuck in the fridge, I was desperate, I wanted him to stop, I wanted him to leave, I needed peace, I was going crazy and it was as if all the years of anguish and pain exploded at that precise moment. I hated him, I really hated him.

The last attack was by no means the worst but it was the one that made me act, I'd had enough!

Two weeks earlier I had walked into my local police station and asked for help after contacting Women's Aid for advice. I was put in touch with the Domestic Violence Unit and from that moment I knew the laws had changed, there was help out there and so when he attacked me I fled straight to the police station.

I want to take this opportunity to thank PC Nathan Spinks who took my statement and ensured I was on the right path when I left the station over 3 hours later. I also want to thank GMP Bolton East Division, from the moment I walked into Astley Bridge Police Station I felt protected and cocooned. Laura Downs, my DV officer, a fantastic young woman who ensured I was strong enough to give evidence. (Laura I hope you are reading this book whilst you are on maternity leave, thank you, thank you so very much you were my rock!) Victim and Witness Support, I really couldn't have done it without your help. You all helped me in your own way and I have you all to thank for where I am now!

My abuser was found guilty of battery after I found the strength to give evidence against him. I filed for divorce and on the 25th May 2011 it was final, I WAS FREE and just as this book has released to the world I will be celebrating my 2nd Divorce Anniversary, double parrrrttttyyyyy!!!!!!!!

The rest is history except that I did have a problem with him when I released Choices-The Darker Years, I guess he doesn't like the content, oh well, tough! I immediately informed the police, he was arrested and charged with breaking the restraining order and appeared in court in January of this year. Unfortunately he was given 60hrs unpaid work for 6 counts of breaking the restraining order which infuriated me so much I began to investigate and subsequently initiated a hopeful change in the laws to protect future victims of domestic violence.

This is my story, okay it's not it all and I know I have rambled so please forgive me but I feel so liberated, so empowered! One day I may just write my biography, who knows..............

I won't be bullied anymore, it's MY life and I make the choices only now they are better ones. I surround myself with good people, people who care about me and support me and I can literally count on one hand the people who I really can trust. Being a victim scarred me, it makes me not trust and every single one of my senses are now heightened and on alert, especially around men. I know that it's sad that I am this way but I will NEVER be abused again, I will NEVER be a victim again.

Earlier this year I was attacked in a most horrible way but this time it wasn't a fist in my face or a broken rib but cyber bullying that left me distraught and ready to jack everything in, yes it was that bad and I want to take this opportunity to address this if I may because I really feel that awareness needs raising.

I joined a site called Goodreads back in November 2012 when The Eyes was released and then as my ideas and projects began to take off I used it to promote both Choices-The Darker Years and this very book. Goodreads has over 14 million users worldwide and is a speciality site for anyone interested in books and so I thought it would be an excellent tool to raise awareness, I was so very wrong. Yes I admit I jumped in feet first in my excitement to spread the word but what followed was horrible as a group of women hounded me, bullied me and attacked me online, I was even threatened with a loaded 38 gun and one woman contacted the refuge that I donate to!

Both The Eyes and Choices-The Darker Years had excellent 5 star reviews but as they continued their assault on me I watched in dismay as both books plummeted and they badly reviewed, many of them admitting that they hadn't even purchased or read the books! If it hadn't of been for some very kind members directing me to another site for help I don't know what I would have done, I do know I wouldn't be typing these words.

Yes I contacted Goodreads and their CEO but they did nothing despite me pointing out that vulgarities as well as threats of violence were being used on their site and they allow children to use it, there reply "we don't moderate it!"

It was horrible and I cried a lot especially when I was mocked for being a victim of domestic violence but after spending a few days with my head down I decided that I would NOT let them win, these women were as bad as my ex husband in my eyes and there was no way I was being a victim again for anyone and I'm glad I didn't hide away as I've always done because then this marvellous book that has helped fifty survivors, yes it's helped me so much too and is going to hopefully raise massive amounts of money for the charities that have been nominated by these brave women and men would not be here! I shall leave you with my very own favourite quote from Choices-The Darker Years.....

"Life is full of choices, chose wisely, chose well." You only get one shot at it and now I plan on living my life to the max, no abuser is going to stop me ever again; no abuser will ever silence me again!

I want to thank the survivors who have participated in this book; you are all so amazing and have inspired me so much. Although I have cried so much whilst putting this book together I have also healed and finally I feel as if I have completed the circle. I feel whole and I have you all to thank for that, I wish I could personally hug each and every one of you.

Dear Reader – thank you so much for spending your money on this book, every single penny will go towards helping victims and survivors. If we can improve the financial status of our charities then we can raise more awareness and hopefully take massive steps to reduce the number of victims of abuse throughout the world.

Domestic violence is something that will not go away on its own, we are going to have to be brutal and take it by the balls and this is the first step in doing that.

#ONEVOICE WILL NEVER BE SILENCED!

SURVIVORS NOT VICTIMS!

Together we stand; together we can make a difference.

Eve x

Website: www.evethomas.co.uk

Twitter: @evethomas40

Email: evethomas@evethomas.co.uk

CHAPTER TWO

Now this very courageous woman's email really piqued my interest but as I read on I was horrified! The author of this story gives her full permission for it to be used to raise awareness and as the lead story in this book. She wishes to remain anonymous and I fully respect her wishes. Her safety is of paramount importance to me and so we have discussed this in detail. I hereby promise that I will under no circumstances reveal her identity, my lips are sealed.

Dear Eve

I noticed on your website that you are looking for stories for your Fifty Shades of Abuse book and I hope you will include mine as my experience started when my partner brought home the Fifty Shades of Grey book.

Before Fifty Shades of Grey we had a "normal relationship." My childhood sweetheart was my Mr Right and I loved him with all my heart. He was kind, gentle, caring and always showered me with affection and love. That was until he brought that book home.

He told me it all started in the office as a laugh, most of the women were reading Fifty and asked him if his girl was reading it too when he replied no they had scoffed and told him to go buy a copy because the sex he would get after it would be unbelievable. Unbelievable isn't the word!

He was all smiles as he walked through the door and into the kitchen, I loved it when he came up behind me and grabbed me around the waist twirling me in his arms until our lips met, he would kiss my cheeks, eyelids and neck whispering how much he had missed me whilst he'd been at work and how much he loved me. He was my man, my special man who loved me as much as I loved him. We had been together for almost 9 years and I trusted him with all my heart.

The previous summer he had whisked me off for a romantic weekend in Paris and whilst having dinner one night in a little restaurant he got down on one knee and proposed.

I was so happy. My childhood sweetheart was to be my husband and the ring he had bought for me was perfect, a single solitaire diamond that sat on a band of white gold and diamonds. It must have cost him a fortune, it was beautiful and that night when we got back to the hotel room he'd sprinkled rose petals all over the bed and there was an ice bucket with a bottle of champagne waiting. That was the best year of my life and we set the date for the following summer. The reason I am telling you all this is because my fiancé was perfect to me, he hardly ever raised his voice, had never hit me, he was a gentleman and always put me first.

As I was putting the plates on the table he was still smiling at me and told me he'd bought me a present, a book. Now I've never been much of a reader but he said it would spice up our sex life and that the girls in work had been talking about the hot character Grey and the "kinky fuckery." We laughed and joked about it over dinner and then he got ready to go out with his mates telling me to have a read if I fancied whilst he was out. My man was a good man and had only ever shown me love and affection so I wanted to do something for him. He earned more money than me and loved buying me gifts but I always felt embarrassed because I couldn't do the same so if I could read this book and it would put some more spice into our sex life then I was up for that besides I didn't really like the fact that he was talking about something I knew nothing about with the girls at work, I guess I was kind of jealous it was about sex after all.

We'd bought books and DVDs to experiment with our sex lives and we had a ball over the years trying out loads of new stuff and had even had a bash at BDSM which had surprised me a lot; I really liked it and found it very easy to switch.

An hour later showered and in my pj's I settled down to begin to read. At first I thought I had the wrong book, where was the hot, sexy stuff this was boring and very badly written too but I soldiered on wanting to please my man. By the time he got home I was fast asleep having got very bored with Fifty Shades of Grey. He was all excited "well have you read it, what do you think?" As I rubbed my eyes I told him that it was boring and I couldn't see what all the fuss was about. He looked disappointed and so I promised to read more, I never got chance.

He stayed up all night and the following morning he rang in sick so he could stay home and finish the book. He hardly spoke to me whilst he was reading except to occasional throw me a funny look. I went to work and left him in the house and when I got home it was then the bombshell came.

"Do you love me?" He asked I was puzzled of course I did. "I want to try some of the stuff that's in this book" he said waving it about in front of me. "It's hot, really hot." I didn't give a shit to be honest, the house was a mess he'd basically sat on his lazy arse all day and read that book whilst I had been to work! I gritted my teeth and smiled making some sarcastic remark about him being a sloth and he immediately jumped up and started vacuuming.

After dinner I went for a shower and whilst I was drying my hair he came into the bedroom and gave me four sheets of paper telling me to read it because it was "fucking sexy!"

Sorry but I didn't find it sexy! When we had dabbled in BDSM and I had been his sub before I had rules to follow but this! When I read what he had wrote on the four sheets of paper that he then asked me to sign I was physically sick – anal fisting, vaginal fisting, what the hell and a set of soft and hard limits that made me feel afraid of the man I had been with since being a wee girl!

He wanted to control me but not in a BDSM way. On his sheets of paper was a contract that he demanded I sign if I didn't then he would withhold all affection from me. I enjoyed our cuddles and kisses, the way he had always adored and cherished me and to try and blackmail me into signing was something I never thought he would do he knew I loved it when he cuddled me whilst I fell asleep why would he want to take that away from me when he said he loved me?

He told me that if a 21 year old virgin in a book could sign then I was pathetic and a wimp if I didn't, he said we had been together a long time and this was just another way of exploring our relationship, trying out new stuff.

I'm really, really ashamed to say I signed after three days of total isolation from him, he meant what he said!

My hell really started then, I wasn't allowed to eat unless he told me to and if I didn't eat then I was punished. The punishments started out with him bending me over his knee and slapping me hard on the bottom but this soon escalated to so much more. I got a urine infection because he wouldn't let me go to the toilet and demanded we have rough sex whilst my bladder was full, (Christian makes Ana do this in Fifty) I was in agony but what was really embarrassing and degrading was when I soiled myself because he wouldn't let me go and empty my bowels and I had an upset stomach, I was punished very severely for the accident despite being ill and he raped me up my bottom he said to teach me a lesson.

I remember going out with my girlfriends one night, he turned up and dragged me home because I had had too much to drink, he then tied my wrists and ankles and raped me over and over again using not only his penis but other objects as well. Yes EL James he raped me! My partner, the love of my life was a good man until he read your book, my partner loved me but he quickly turned into an abuser just like your character Christian Grey. I can never forgive Fifty Shades or you EL James, you turned my lovely, kind, gentleman into a monster who seemed to enjoy raping and beating me. He would often quote your book using it to belittle me or to get his own way although I don't think I ever quite lived up to your 21 year old virgin in the oral sex department! When I vomited because he was choking me with his penis I was told I was fucking useless because Ana managed it and she was a virgin! Thank you E L James, thank you so much.

It went on for almost 6 months but I finally got free but I will forever bear the scars that Fifty Shades of Grey left me with, emotional scars and physical scars and for that I have you to thank. It wouldn't be so bad if you admitted that your so called romantic lead man was an abuser and it scares me that all these women think he's their ideal man. Trust me he is not! After my partner read Fifty Shades of Grey he was no longer interested in being my equal he wanted to completely control me, if I went to my mother's he followed me, he manipulated me, punished me and controlled me. Your book destroyed my relationship, destroyed the boy I had known since being a little girl. I was too afraid to go the police and every night I have to take medication so I can sleep. E L James don't defend Grey, he is an abuser plain and simple.

Thank you Eve for allowing me to share my story with you. I hope it helps to raise awareness for domestic violence and abuse but also that Christian Grey is an abuser and that Fifty Shades Of Grey is NOT a love story its abuse wearing the disguise of romance. I am still a victim but you have helped me so much and I know that one day soon I will wake up a survivor, thank you so very much for giving me this opportunity, you were right, writing does help!

Message from Eve – This was a very chilling story to read but one that confirmed that this book is very much needed. I hope you one day find your peace but until then know that you are not alone and I will help you in anyway I can. You have shown a great deal of bravery in sharing your story, thank you. I hope that writing has empowered you. Eve x

CHAPTER THREE
A survivor's story.

Dear Eve

As promised, here's my story:

I met my abuser in 1991 he was charming and paid me so much attention and wanted to spend every minute with me. I a shy and probably naive 19 year old who had not had a boyfriend before found this wonderful and thought I had found my Prince Charming. How wrong I was.

Our relationship moved very quickly, and within a few weeks we were engaged. He would tell me that I was his soul-mate, that he knew that he wanted to spend the rest of his life with me; I was drawn into his beliefs and was totally under his spell.

He quickly caused a rift in my family resulting in me leaving my parents' home and becoming totally reliant on him, even though he was not working and did not get paid employment for the entire duration of our marriage.

After a period of living between his mother's and his brother's homes we eventually got our own flat. By this time I had not had contact with my family for weeks on end, and did not see any of my friends. Once we were living together I finally saw the real him.

It started with him choosing my clothes; how I did my hair, what we ate... he was in control of everything. I assumed that this is what a proper relationship was, I didn't know anything else.

He was physically abusive as well, but not very often at the start, and he would sometimes apologise and blame stress for what he did to me. He told me that with my help he would change, and I believed him, I thought that I could change him.....so so wrong.

Eventually we had our first child, a son. I was very ill during my pregnancy and had to go into hospital for 6 weeks, this was due to stress on myself and the fact that I was still working and he would only give me a few pounds to get my lunch but would call me at work asking me to bring cigarettes home with me when I finished. I by then knew what mood he would be in if I didn't so I would not have anything for lunch and use my lunch money to get his cigarettes, even though he was home all day with my money, and he couldn't be bothered to go and buy his own cigarettes. When I got home I would also have to work for him on an internet business he was trying to set up and he would make me work until 2-3am while pregnant knowing I had to get up at 8am to go to work.

I hoped that after our son was born that he would change....it only made him worse and as each child came along, 4 in total he became more controlling, and more abusive, physically and verbally.

There are too many incidents to recall, and I am sure that some of them I have blanked from my mind because there were so many.

The last few years of our marriage were the worst. He would not allow the children to go to school telling them that he was bullied at school and the same would happen to them. He kept us totally isolated; only his family were allowed to visit. If I wanted to see my family, I would have to see them at my mum's home and was given a time limit. He would call me constantly while I was there, making me tell them lies to pretend that his business was really successful when it was in fact not making any money at all and by now he had me working from 9am to 3am the next morning 7 days a week. I hardly had any chance to educate the children from home so they were not getting a proper education and practically had to bring themselves up.

Life was not even a life, we existed. The children would get up each morning and ask me what mood their father was in.

We were always on eggshells because he could go from happy and cheerful to incredibly violent within a few minutes. We had to watch what we said and did in front of him. He was also physically abusive towards the children pushing them around, hitting them, swearing at them and putting them down. When he was in one of his 'demonic moods' as he called them, he would make us all sit down and listen to him. This could sometimes go on for hours with him telling us that he was all we had, that my family didn't care about us, that we were nothing and would still be nothing without him.

He also told me that if I ever left him, (and believe me I had taken the kids a few times and left with them over the years but he always apologised and charmed me back promising it wouldn't happen again but it always did) he would come after me and make sure that nobody else would ever want me and that if my family got involved he would kill them all. I stayed because I knew his families reputation, I knew that they were the type of people who would do it.

20 years I put up with it, I never told my family what was happening I was

ashamed that I had allowed this to happen and in another way I think that I did not want to admit to being a 'battered-wife'. It all finally came out when a friend I had not seen since school got in touch with my via Facebook and I think because they were not directly involved I just poured my heart out to him and told him everything that had gone on. He was horrified and told me that I needed to leave my husband.

I left on 9th July 2010. My eldest daughter had a dental appointment and while there I called my husband's brother and told him I couldn't go through this anymore, I wanted him out of the house.

He went to my home and took my husband to his home. Then the mind games started. He would call me from the roof of the brother's flats, saying that he should jump off and then I could be free. He started drinking and told me that he would end up an alcoholic on the streets if I left him. His mother also threatened to come after my family if anything happened to him so I reluctantly took him back. It was then that his paranoia set in.

He convinced himself that my family were going to come after him, he would take our mobile phones and lock all the doors so that we could not have contact with anyone or leave the home, me and my children were hostage in our own home. Then he threatened suicide trying to drink rat-poison and on one occasion, put a knife into my 13 year old daughters hand and told her to kill him....unbeknown to him, I had hidden a phone in the bathroom and texted my sister to let her know what was going on. Then my family stepped in and got social services involved.

At first I was angry because I was afraid that my children would be taken away but as time went by and demands were made of him from social services I could see that it was the best thing they ever did for me. He was asked to have domestic violence therapy, he refused. He would not engage with social services and denied the abuse and said I was exaggerating. It was when he said that no-one could ever make him leave and that he would do something to go down in history like killing himself and me and the children that I knew how dangerous the situation was. With the help of my social worker and a police officer, on January 14th 2011, we managed to get out of the house while he was at a mental health assessment. We stayed in temporary accommodation for a week while I got a non-molestation order to have him removed from my home. Within a week me and the children were back home without him there. He was not allowed to make any form of contact.

My children are now in full time education and doing really well. Our home is a noisy, chaotic home, but it is also a happy home and I started divorce proceedings. Me and my children have all had to have therapy and the problems are still on-going but getting better. My children are all I have now been divorced for 1 year and the children have no contact with their father and do not wish to see him. He has taken me to court for access to the younger two aged 6 and 8 but so far the case is going well and cafcass are going to recommend no contact as he had contact before and did not comply with the rules and cancelled contact himself. He has also been told to have therapy but only attended one session where he showed himself to be aggressive, violent and intimidating.

Life for me and my children has totally changed, we still have issues with knowing who to trust and my teenage children will not go out by themselves after the isolation they suffered but we are working on that. I am happy being single, and do not know if I could ever have another relationship because as I well know men can appear to be charming and loving, but abusive men do this as well to gain your trust and then treat you as slaves and a prisoner in your own home, you become their punch bag, verbally and physically and I know that I never want to be in that situation again.

Thank you for listening, thank you for including my story I hope it helps others. Marie wanted me to add this message to future printings of this wonderful book. My name is Marie Knightley in the first printing I remained anon but on receiving a copy of the book I felt empowered enough to stand up and say "Hey I'm Marie, I'm chapter 3 and I'm a SURVIVOR of domestic violence and abuse.

Message from Eve - This story really moved and reminded me so much of my own life. You are a brave, brave lady and thank you so much for allowing us into your past. May your journey as a survivor continue and I hope that like me you found the healing powers of writing whilst you shared your story. Good luck with the future to you and your children. Eve x

p.s. You will only find this additional message in this print of #OneVoice Fifty Shades Of Abuse – CONGRATULATIONS to Marie, you are a very, very courageous woman and it was with such joy and big smiles when you decided to unveil your beautiful face and identity. You are a STAR, GO YOU!!!!!Hugs x

CHAPTER FOUR

I am proud to say that I met this gentleman on the Chelsea Krost Show, he was a guest that this amazing, young woman was interviewing and whilst I was listening from across the pond I asked if she would put me in touch with him. You may be asking why was this particular man significant, the answer he is a SURVIVOR of domestic abuse. Marvellous Chelsea weaved her magic and by the end of his interview we were in touch!

My story

I was 21 when I ended a short engagement to a girl my parents liked more than I did. Perhaps it was the emotion of being "attached" that made me want to jump right back into another relationship. I met a girl a bit older than myself and she had just come out of a very abusive relationship. In my naivety I thought I would show this girl that she deserved a good guy, that I would take care of her and bandage her wounds like I had just found some bird with a wounded wing. She however was feeling her biological clock ticking louder and the two of us married quickly. It wasn't long before I realized you can't fix someone else, you can't give someone a sense of self worth. Soon after we married we had a daughter. Even though neither of us was happy in our relationship we decided that divorce was not an option since it was so prevalent in both of our families. I was acting in theatre companies when we met, a young actor with big dreams. She quickly put an end to that as she indicated she did not want me acting as she did not want me having that close a relationship with a female actress. Since I thought that loving someone meant putting their desires above your own, I quit the theatre and got a 9-5 job. The next thing she wanted gone was my truck followed by much of my wardrobe, it seemed as if I was slowly losing the things I identified with as she tried to change me into someone she liked more. While she changed the outward appearances it was the inward feelings about myself and my identity that slowly died.   While I made good money to support our children and allow her to stay home my job was influenced by the economy. It wasn't long into our marriage that my first lay off occurred. Since I wasn't allowed to even see the check book, I had no idea where the money I was making went to. There surely wasn't any in reserve to hold us over till the next job. So, we lost everything. It wasn't enough to suffer the emotional trauma of losing every material possession but to have my wife call me a "failure" only sunk me deeper into a depression about the situation and she quickly began seeking, although in secret, a more successful man.

The word "stupid" was used so many times that for the longest time after our relationship ended the hearing of that word would send me to a place I didn't like. Another popular phrase used by her while together was "you're lucky you have me because nobody else would want you." Every subsequent relationship that didn't last only served to re-enforce these words. The result was a lack of caring about who I dated; I dated girls I had no business dating some of which I never even introduced to my children. It was a pattern of one self destructive relationship after another. My mind, knew the reasons they didn't work was they were not the right ones but my heart still felt unworthy of someone better. The girls that left me for a richer man only re-enforced those feelings of inadequacy and eventually made me stop dating all together. After one such girl quickly went back to her abusive ex worth lots of money I voluntarily went to counseling offered at my church to seek the reasons I was stuck in this pattern. Seems, it goes back to my early childhood and an event that involved my mother, an event where I felt I needed to protect her and guard over her. Though many early childhood memories are suppressed or long forgotten there is one event that I recall vividly. It was the words from a neighbour blaming my mother's illness on my brother and I being such "bad boys" that I over compensated and made sure I took care of her. I was her little guardian as my father was often overseas as a Marine. My counselor indicated this gave me a "rescue mentality" and I found girls who needed to be "rescued" since I couldn't solve my mother's issues.

Verbal, emotional and psychological abuse victims do not show the same injuries that physical abuse victims do though the injuries and scars are just as real. Criminal charges are impossible against the abuser since there are no visible signs of injury. Verbal, emotional and psychological abuse happens slowly over a period of time in a way that often the victim doesn't even know its happening.

I learned a lot in those counseling sessions how to recognize the "red flags" in someone that prevents me from being the hero. I found that knowing my self worth attracted those who appreciated the best in me. While I am still on the search for the "right girl" I at least can recognize the "wrong" ones and knowing my self worth, know that I only deserve one that appreciates me just as I am. It took many years to re-gain my true self. The friends and family that stood close by my side, including my ex's family have allowed me to see myself in a better light. I no longer react to the word "Stupid" as I did and knowing I can recognize the people that will only serve to tear me down allows me to be happy by myself, while I search for someone. I feel one should not look for someone to "complete" them but for someone who "compliments" them, someone who will take the time to get to know your deepest emotions, accept you, scars and all. It became obvious that trying to date anyone while hiding behind the walls we build to protect ourselves only results in failure as the other person can only see the parts of us we allow. When we take our walls down and become vulnerable, finding our self worth and allowing others to see us can they fall in love with us as a whole person. Now, I find the more open I am about who I am and my experiences I make deeper connections with others. It takes time to allow oneself to trust another person again, having those around you that know your story and history helps.

Message from Eve - Thank you so much for sharing your story which reinforces that men as well as women are affected by domestic violence/domestic abuse, it takes a very brave man to step forward the way you have. I hope one day not too far away you find your "special lady," she's out there somewhere just waiting. Thank you. Eve x

CHAPTER FIVE

I'm not too sure how to do this – how to start it or whether it is going to be enough.

My story starts when I was 13. This was the first time I was abused/touched inappropriately. It was by someone in my class in senior school, he was in my form class and I guess you could say he was kind of like my boyfriend. My best friend Rose was going out with his cousin. We'd all met up one Sunday afternoon and were just wandering round town. At some point it started to rain and the lads decided we should take shelter in a large clearing of trees near the edge of the town centre. We thought nothing of it and followed them in. As soon as we were in deep enough to not be seen from the road we were separated from one another. Craig took me off to one part and Rose got taken off to a different part where I couldn't see her. If that wasn't bad enough Craig started trying to grope at my breasts, I kept pushing him away but he didn't want to stop. I tried shouting for Rose but as soon as I did he started to kiss me to muffle the noise. He then grabbed my wrists behind me and started pulling at my jeans with his other hand. I was really frightened at this point and was shaking while all the time trying to get away from him. I don't know how he did it but he managed to get his hand down the front of my jeans and started to wiggle his fingers under my knickers. I clamped my thighs together tightly but he kicked my legs apart, as a fell forward a little he managed to get his fingers inside me. I started crying and he just kissed at my tears. I've no idea what happened to Rose at this point and was past thinking of her. He fingered me for quite some time (or so it felt) while I cried and let him.

Once he'd had enough he pulled his hand out and shoved his fingers in my mouth. He told me the next time we were alone he was going to do this and more to me but I was never planning on being alone with him ever again! He tidied me up a bit and shouted for his cousin. Rose didn't seem to be upset or anything and we just said goodbye to them and went off home. This was before mobile phones were commonplace so we couldn't just ring someone for help or to let people know where we were. Our parents had been out looking for us as they were obviously worried. We sat in the car together not speaking about anything that had happened and just let our parents tell us off the whole time. I sat there not knowing what to do - what to say. Would I be believed? Could I say anything? Would it get me in trouble all the more? I just chose to not breathe a word - it was easier. I felt ashamed, dirty and used but at the time I wasn't sure of what those feelings were. How was I to know? Both Rose & I didn't have to have a lot of contact with these boys ever again, apart from hearing his name at registration. I found out a few years later that I was the third girl he'd done that too and the girl after me was raped by him. I suppose I should be thankful it wasn't me that was raped. Rose never spoke once to me about it and we never have since. Following that incident news spread amongst the boys that I was an easy target... boys would ask to go out with me and assume they could treat me in the same way. I never let them and managed to work out quickly that they were only after a quick fondle. One boy I went out with thought it would be fun to touch my breasts (I have always been heavy set) while kissing me. I didn't want him to in the slightest, not when I was discovering my body myself. As I wouldn't let him do what he wanted he broke things off calling me names. A lucky escape? Perhaps.

I was 15 years old and had to attend a wedding when I first came across Doug. He was an usher (grooms attendant) and showed us to our seats. I smiled at him and said thank you (manners have always been ingrained into me) and I thought no more of it. He was at the reception and spoke with my mum & me briefly. He asked me to dance at the evening reception and I agreed. I wasn't interested in him in any way but he was nice enough to chat with. A few days after the wedding he rang me at home (I didn't give him my number but another family member did) and asked me to meet him after he'd finished his swimming lesson. I said no and he said that he'd keep on asking me until I gave in and said yes. I thought he was joking but he kept ringing the house every day and after a week I agreed to meet him just to shut him up. I don't know how it happened but I ended up being his girlfriend. He was very good at getting me to do what he wanted without me realising I was even doing it. After a few weeks I said something in passing to him and he slapped me hard across the face, I was in shock and didn't respond at all to it. How are you supposed to respond to a slap across the face? Yes people reading may say "well I'd not stand for it" it's not that easy though. Until you've been there and experienced something for yourself you can never say "well I'd do A, B or C". From then on if he felt I spoke out of turn he'd hit me - usually a slap to start with and then a punch or a bite; though he'd never do it where the bruises would be visible to others. It was difficult trying to hide the marks when I was in school especially for PE as all the girls changed together. I used to dread those days most of all but if anyone noticed they never said anything to me and I'm not sure what I would have done had someone asked me. I remember playing badminton in school once with cracked ribs and trying to just continue on as normal. As it was my first proper relationship I couldn't ask anyone if the things I was going through were normal – who could I ask? Who was there to turn to?

We had spoken about sex as I was learning all about sex education in school (it was quite new to the education system in those days). But he knew that I wanted to wait until I got married before going down that particular path. He had previously agreed and said we should wait. For one thing I was in no way mentally prepared for intercourse never mind physically ready for the next step. I wasn't at a stage where I trusted him enough with my body for that. We were in my bedroom at home and my mum was asleep in her room as she had a migraine. There was a film on the TV in the background and he laid me on the bed and started to touch me, all over. I kept telling him my mum was in the next room & would hear us but he wasn't backing down. I remember him pulling at my trousers and knickers and me fighting him off but he put his hand round my throat & started to strangle me. He whispered in my ear to do as I was told or he'd cut me if I didn't (he always carried a pocket knife with him) so I stopped fighting and let him do as he wished. I don't remember a lot of what occurred during the attack but it felt as if it lasted hours. I remember feeling a number of things during and after it: pain, fear, and confusion. Once he'd finished he told me I'd have to make an appointment at the doctors for the morning after pill. I'd never been to the gp's without my mum before so had to sneak of school the following day to ask the doctor for this tablet with mixed feelings. I didn't know or understand what it would do to me or why I needed to take it and all the doctor wanted to do was lecture me for underage sex. I didn't have underage sex: I was raped you stupid woman!

Following that incident he would have sex with me anytime he could. I would try to make excuses about being on my period or that we couldn't be together but he always managed to find a way for us to be alone. I would try to wear trousers thinking that he'd be less inclined to try and never wore makeup like my other friends of the same age. Anything to throw him off but none of it worked. I became more withdrawn and would just hide out in my bedroom at home, staying away from all of the family in case they noticed and asked me something. I wasn't sure how I could keep all of these things in and was scared at what would happen to me if I couldn't. Doug was very "persuasive" with sex....as I said he carried a pocket knife and I have scars all over my body where he would cut me with his knife if I didn't act how he wished or did as I was told. I have them on my stomach, thighs, pubic bone, arms and two sets of his initials carved into my left wrist & right ankle bone. He once told me that I would belong to him forever as I had his mark on me.

He was a scout leader too and I was with him at a meeting one night, helping out in the kitchen. I was getting a drink for him & me and chatting with one of his friends who happened to tell a joke as Doug walked into the room. He took it that I was flirting with his friend (which I wasn't) and whispered in my ear that he'd teach me a lesson later on for flirting when we were alone. I tried to shrug it off but knew I'd be in for a beating as I could see his eyes cloud over with anger.

Nothing I said would alleviate the situation and I just shut up and hung my head. We ended up going back to his friend's house instead of going back to Doug's but he looked as if he'd calmed down so I thought he'd forgotten all about the earlier incident. I was yet again; in the kitchen -getting drinks for everyone when he came in behind me as I'd taken "too long" to get the drinks for us. He dragged me out of the kitchen by my hair (which was mid shoulder length) and dragged me all the way into the front room as I was screaming for him to let me go. He started to kick me in the stomach and hit me repeatedly telling me how I'd have to be taught a big lesson this time for messing up and flirting with his friends.......... He started to rape me in front of all his friends and then told them to join in. There were 5 of them there but one left me alone. I was pinned down at my wrists and ankles while they took it in turns with me in all manner of ways. I was forced to perform oral sex while others raped me not knowing who was using me or when it was going to end. In the end I remember floating above my body - trying to will myself to not be there and prey that it would all be over with as soon as possible. I stopped crying as I became numb to it all and I think Doug thought I was enjoying myself. When they'd finished he had each one of them put a cigarette out on my back so I had a "constant reminder from being a slut". He made me thank every one of them for using me like that before I re-dressed and he took me back over to his house to wait for my life home. I got into the car and didn't speak about any of it.

The end of the relationship came after the most brutal attack I've ever suffered. I was having a sleep at home after preparing Sunday lunch for the family as I used to help out quite a lot due to various home factors. He was sent up to my room as my father assumed I was revising for my mock exams for school. All I knew was waking up to him lying on top of me with my hands held above my head & all his weight on me, him already having sex with me. I couldn't breathe and didn't know where the f**k I was. By the time I'd come round properly he had flipped me over and started to do it all over again (he used to like to play around with positions as he knew it scared me). When he had finished and was satisfied I went to the bathroom to clean myself up. As I walked back through the door he grabbed me; slammed the door shut and punched me so hard in my stomach that it pushed me over to the bed. He started to kick me repeatedly in the stomach and was saying how he would make sure I would never carry his children - I didn't know what he was on about - and I didn't care much either. When he grew tired of hurting me, I managed to excuse myself from him saying I was going for a shower as we were due to visit his friend again that evening (to the very same house I'd been gang raped in). I locked myself in the bathroom, ran the shower & curled up in a ball at the bottom of it crying my eyes out hoping no-one would hear me. I knew I couldn't carry on like this for much longer and attempted to take my own life with a razor, I slit at my wrists but just as I had started to cut one wrist he started banging on the door telling me to hurry up and get out. Being so used to following his voice I did as I was told. As he'd calmed down some he finally managed to tell me that the last condom he had used (he always used them) had split & he "had to beat me to kick any potential chance at having his child out". I told him I wasn't feeling too well and would he mind if I stayed home that night. He agreed thankfully and left me at home. He returned a few days later and broke things off with me saying how I was too clingy and needy and that he couldn't cope as he felt too restricted!! A few days later I suffered a miscarriage -evidently I was carrying his child though a lot further along than he would ever have anticipated (I was about 8 weeks as I could make out a little prawn in all the blood). I dealt with the trauma of that alone as well as all the beatings, verbal & mental abuse and the rapes too as I had no-one I could talk to. My parents couldn't know as it would break their hearts, my brother was too young to speak with. I guess I wasn't really ready to work out exactly what had happened to me throughout that relationship either. In the months that followed the end of that relationship I grew withdrawn and depressed - as you might imagine. I hid myself away as much as possible and stayed away from boys for fear of what would happen to me.

A few months later I was visiting a friend who had been kicked out of his home by his mother. He had asked for help as he was feeling down. We chatted and he ended up getting me quite drunk on cider. I ended up telling him some of what had happened with Doug. He suggested he help me with it and told me to lie on his bed - I was very drunk and feeling sleepy by this point - he told me he would be gentle with me and would help me "get over it". He lifted my top and saw my scarred stomach but kissed it instead of freaking out like I imagined he would. He gently took my trousers down and kissed my thighs, then he removed my knickers and I freaked. I didn't want him touching me down there or doing anything to me but I couldn't speak - I started to cry and shake but he kept on kissing & touching me. He got on top of me and started to have sex with me telling me what to do & how to move. I was doing as I was told while still crying and couldn't believe I was agreeing to it all. He finished and covered me up with his quilt and told me to rest. I didn't know what to think and lay there for a bit with my head swimming. After some time passed I got up and left him. Luckily my aunt only lived 10 minutes away so I staggered to her house before she sobered me up and took me home. I was grounded for drinking when I shouldn't but I never told my parents what had happened to me that night. I still am unsure if I consented or not though but it didn't feel right to me and makes me feel bad now as I write.

Two years later I happened to meet up with a lad I'd been in school with and had always had a thing for. He was lovely and we ended up staying together for 7 years. He never hurt me once but as I was trying to deal with all the trauma of the abuse I caused lots of arguments between us. He couldn't cope with my constant mood swings and depression and as I started to trust him more, my walls started to come down. As time went on I started having flashbacks and panic attacks. That's when I started to self harm. Every time I felt out of control with a situation I would cut myself, it would give me an instant feeling of peace and I would know I was alive as I could see my blood pumping. I could control my own body - feel the cut stinging or see my blood to know I was actually alive and could feel "something". I attended counselling and had a CPN assigned to me. I was on heavy anti-depressants but nothing seemed to be working and I again attempted suicide. I was 23 when I had my second attempt at this but my boyfriend found me and took me to A&E where they pumped my stomach. I took time off work and undertook more intense counseling to try to come to terms with the abuse. During the time when I was having counseling I'd built up such a wall around myself to keep me safe I couldn't see that it was starting to all fall apart. I ended up in a very bad spiral self harming, going out drinking and crying constantly, unsure of how to deal with everything. I split up with my boyfriend and decided to remain single, it was safer for me. If I was single no-one would ever hurt me again. No-one would ever suffer from my terrible moods or have to listen to me cry and blame myself I met my husband quite by chance – through a mutual friend and things got off to a good start. We went out for meals together and flirted with one another. We didn't really discuss any of my history as I didn't think we'd have a serious relationship. I didn't see him in that way at all. Yes he was good looking and we had a laugh but I wasn't looking for anything serious or heavy. One afternoon I was at his place and we were messing around. We started to talk about sex and he took off his belt and wrapped it round my neck…… he started pulling me closer to him and I ended up on all fours, I was so turned on by it but couldn't understand why. After that we started to experiment in the bedroom and I became his bedroom slave. I'd wear certain things for him and would wear a collar around my neck – he would be the Master and I'd be his slave. This only started out as a bit of bedroom fun but ended up flowing over into our day to day lives. I felt so free and didn't have the usual feelings of guilt or hate at myself when we had sex. I felt good. I was enjoying myself! It just flowed over into our everyday lives and I'd do certain set things for him every day. He would always buy me presents and treats if I'd behaved well – a bit of positive reinforcement I guess. Unfortunately things went bad after I had our first child. He became verbally abusive with me and would tell me much of the same things that Doug used to tell me. I started to believe it all –

again – and was so run down with post natal depression that I closed off to everyone around me. I was really low, I was suicidal low but I refused to leave my baby. He started to drink more and more but as I come from a family of non-drinkers I didn't know there was a problem hiding in plain sight. We'd still have good days and would have the bedroom M/s as I wanted – I'd be happy and free. And then the abuse would start again. I got pregnant a second time (4 years later) and things just got worse from there. He never wanted the second child – and wanted me to abort her. I refused. I was not prepared to make a life and then kill it – not after miscarrying when I was younger. I suffered throughout the pregnancy and he was aggressive, violent and drunk through most of it. He was that out of it when I gave birth he doesn't even remember being there. After we married (yes I was stupid enough to marry him) just before the birth of our second child things got worse. He would demand sex all the time. If I refused he would still continue anyway. He would hurt me where no-one would see the marks, much like Doug but the emotional abuse was the worst. I was suffering badly and no-one knew. Not until I had him arrested for breaking my ribs and strangling me. It was over something so stupid (for not ordering a Chinese for dinner one evening). Because I'd told him about Doug – as our relationship changed he was aware of my history and the words used by Doug so he knew (and still knows) *how* to hurt me – what words hurt the most. He is physically abusive and will dig his nails into me leaving marks and cuts – but always something that looks as if its been done accidentally – or something that looks as if I could have done it to myself. If he drinks a lot (which is most of the time) he will also touch me and try to force himself onto me, it happens more than I'd care to admit to and makes me feel so ashamed of myself for staying. I've never left him, even though I wish I could... I have no-where to go. Nowhere safe for me & my children. Who would believe what's happened to me? Who would believe me after everything else I've been through?

As to my life now…............... well I realised when he & I messed around with BDSM in the bedroom that there was something I needed to explore. Something I felt was missing from my life.

BDSM, isn't all about "yes sir, no sir, three bags full sir" stuff – its having someone care for you and set you rules to help keep you safe. It's nothing like the 50 shades of grey books although some of it – such as the "sex scenes" can occur. Having a Master is all about ensuring someone's happiness, making you available to him for his pleasure in whatever way he wishes – that doesn't always translate into sex. It could be from making Him his favourite dish, getting him drinks etc..... A Master wishes to care for his slave, to ensure their safety that they are comforted when needed, looked after and loved. I was lucky enough to find someone to mentor me, someone who was willing to take me under their wing, someone who was kind enough to set me a few rules and guide me. This I did for a few months until I came across a Master who was gracious enough to take me on as His. I am lucky to now have my own Master who provides all of that for me as well as gives me the rules and guidance I need. He protects me from harm – from myself, from the harm of others and ensure He is happy by doing as He wishes. I carry out everything set for me to the best of my abilities and will always ensure He is happy – if he isn't and I'm failing then He gives me direction and helps me. I have rules in a contract – which are always adhered to. If I fail, I'm punished. Not beaten to a pulp or anything, but corrected - much like you do with a child. You learn from your mistakes so it doesn't happen again. Master is always gracious and accepts an apology and will always ensure I am safe and cared for after my punishment is over. He always tells me that I am forgiven as often I tend to not forgive myself when I have misbehaved. Luckily this has only happened on 3 occasions. I love my Master, He means the world to me and I am lucky to belong to Him. As one of my close friends said to me yesterday "the fact that M/s relationships are for the most part abuse free whereas abuse occurs so regularly in vanilla relationships is a paradox that needs explaining. That plus the fact that D/s is entirely consensual and a sub can walk away anytime they wish. Can't always do that in vanilla ones!" That is the difference between my relationship with my Master, whom I adore to that of my husband who I should love but can't.

Message from Eve – Your story really got to me and I reached out to you, you have a friend in me and I will do everything I can to help you become free and happy at last. Smiles and laughter are not that far away, have faith. Eve x

CHAPTER SIX

May I introduce a VERY, brave young woman, she is amazing!

My Voice

Well I didn't expect to be going through a domestic violence based relationship at such a young age so I will tell you how it all started.

I was only sixteen when I met him, he found me on Facebook on a group page for people with BBM'S to meet new people. (BBM is the Blackberry Messenger Service) We started talking and I met him with a friend that also knew him. My friend never told me how she met him but at the time I really didn't think anything of it all.

Me and my friend met him and we spent the day in Stockport town centre and he said he would come back to Marple with us. Whilst we were waiting for the bus he pulled up his trackies and he had a kitchen knife stuffed down his sock, I was scared I was going to get stabbed or something but he explained it was because he had been jumped and didn't what that to happen again, it was his protection so I believed him.

After time we got together and I thought he was a nice guy and wouldn't hurt me because he understood me. He met my mum and put on his nice guy charm but she never liked him even from that first time she met him, she had a gut feeling something was wrong.

A few months passed and he started to act weird, he'd say "it's me and you versus the world" and he loved me and didn't want to loose me to anyone. He started getting me to stay at his house and then I wouldn't want to go home because he would threaten me that the relationship would be over if I did.

He then started to take all my friends away from me by causing trouble, telling me that nobody liked me and that all my female friends were chatting him up on Facebook.

One morning I was woken up by him pulling me out of my bed by my hair, I was so scared I didn't think he could be so nasty. While he cooked tea later on that night I was stood in the kitchen and he put a knife to my throat, he claimed he was "playing" but I wanted my mum so bad, he really scared me.

A couple of weeks passed and he started pinching my knee caps and hitting me on the back of my knees, putting me to the floor. I didn't understand why but it always seemed to be just one knee.

We used to argue a lot, he'd always say to me "you are not a good girlfriend you still speak to your ex," "You won't find anyone better than me." Yes, I still spoke to my ex but he is my friend.

I thought that if my boyfriend loved me then why was he controlling what I do, where I go, who I see etc. He wouldn't let me go with him when he went to my house to get my clothes; I was left locked in his flat alone with nobody to talk to.

We split up a couple of months later following an argument because I caught him out chatting my old friend's up. He got angry and kicked me out of his flat at 2am in the morning and as I was walking to a friend's I was crying thinking I want my mum to just come and save me....... if only she knew what I was really doing that night.

On my 18th birthday I was spending the day with my family so I turned off my phone for the day, he came up at 10pm, stayed for about 15 minutes telling me about some other girl he had met while he was in Buxton called Jazz, trying to make me jealous. He gave me my card and a kiss and a hug goodbye and disappeared.

The next day he started having a go at me again so I turned my phone off only to turn it on a few hours later and find a picture of him chatting with some other girl, arranging to meet her at weekend to have sex with her.

I'd had enough. I'd come home with bruises where he'd pinched and punched my legs, I needed help and so eventually I came out with it all and told my mum.

I ended it for good! 8th May 2013 is my escape date and I am proud of it! Now I have an injunction to keep him away from me.

I couldn't be any more stronger and happier than I am today and I just wanted to share my story of my abuse and to let others know they are not alone, so stay strong!!!

Danielle Butler

I would like to nominate Stockport Without Abuse and give permission for you to use my story in your book.

Message from Eve – I welcomed Danielle's story with open arms as I feel that it conveys a very important message that has not been covered in this book of true stories. A young girl, an innocent using social media to find friends, Facebook in particular found not a friend but a violent and sadistic abuser. I fully support Danielle in her wishes and I'm so happy that she has come forward and wants to stand with me raising awareness. WE WILL DO THIS, THE ABUSE MUST STOP. I hope that anyone thinking of using the internet to meet people does so safely, please ensure any location software is turned off, please protect yourselves. I now invite you to read the next chapter from her mum, a woman that lived every minute of the abuse with her brave daughter. You both have my upmost respect. We will take this journey together, we will make a difference. Hugs brave and beautiful lady. X

CHAPTER SEVEN

Becoming a parent is one of the happiest days of your life full of love, hope and expectations. Watching them take their first everything is truly amazing and then they grow up.

Never in a million years did I ever expect my daughter Danielle to get involved with a bully, a violent abuser. First the bruises began to show then he started the mind games, the emotional abuse, the calling of nasty names.

"You don't need anyone else," "Only I care for you," "You're fat, ugly, slag, bitch." The names go on and listening to her scream "I hate you" and walking out of the house at midnight to be with him I knew the control was there.

I cried myself to sleep at night searching my memories to where I went wrong what did I do that was so bad for this to happen. Sometimes I just wanted to curl up and never wake up because the pain I felt is unbearable, helpless not knowing if she's safe.

I am doing some counselling training and I believe everyone can change if they really want to accept responsibility but no he acts like the world owes him. He's hard done to, he doesn't understand why we don't like him, he hasn't done anything wrong it's all Danielle, it's her fault. Her head was completely messed up being abused physically and emotionally, believing she's not worth anything, it broke my heart.

Danielle moved out for two months and we stopped speaking. I lost all the fight I had in me it was easier to forget what was happening or at least try to pretend it wasn't happening. For us denial is not a good place to be it's not real but it didn't last long. I heard Danielle had nowhere to go because he kicked her out and so I asked her to come home but before she did they got back together. A week later he ended it again but I didn't dare raise my hopes of her coming home so she could be safe because I expected her to go running back.

Things were different this time she rang the police, she wanted him to stop and leave her alone, finally a light at the end of the tunnel, dare I hope?

Listening to Danielle making a statement hearing about his 'toy fights,' him choking her whilst having sex, locking her outside in the dark with no phone so she couldn't phone me. Whilst my daughter, my baby was giving her statement she turned and said "I was so scared mummy." Another part of me died I wasn't there to protect her, my child. Him telling her no one would want her, hitting her pressure points in her neck and laughing are all too much and at 17 years old she shouldn't have been going through all that but finally the end the police arrested him surely we could start to put it behind us.

Christmas came and went New Year we toasted to new beginnings, lessons learnt and said goodbye to 2012. We brought in 2013 to new beginnings and prayed that Danielle would become happy again. He can rot!

Two whole months then my world came crashing down, my life came to a standstill, my daughter went back to him I wanted to die after the police told us they weren't taking any further action.

It took him 2 weeks then she walked out telling me she hated me, the look in her eyes told me she meant it my heart was shattered. I couldn't sleep properly I cried all the time, I just wanted my baby home but she wouldn't speak to me, she didn't want to come home because he wouldn't let her in case she didn't go back to him. She's my baby, I'm supposed to protect her yet there was nothing I could do to help her. I felt so powerless, empty and lost.

Danielle was back and forth between home and his, he couldn't totally break the bond we share and the nights I couldn't sleep Danielle was being hurt. She came home with an injured knee that was the time she came home for good. I prayed a lot for this day to come and it did and on the day after her 18th birthday, 8th May 2013 it ended for good. I did think she would go back like always but this time Danielle was different, stronger. Ehen she applied for an injunction I knew then this chapter was coming to an end.

I just want all parents to know it can happen to anyone and it's not your fault the blame should stay with the abuser - Anna McCullock

I Anna McCullock give permission for you to use my story in you book and would like to nominate Stockport Against Abuse, the same charity as my beautiful daughter to receive my share of the total profits.

Thank you.

Message from Eve – Anna your story moved me so much. As a mum myself and also a survivor I can only imagine the pain and distress not to mention heart break that you suffered. I am so happy that Danielle is free and safe now and I thank you both for sharing your stories. May smiles, laughter and happiness follow you both always. Eve x

CHAPTER EIGHT

What's the chance of getting involved with an abuser? I now know that 1 in 4 and 1 in 6 men will.

I had a "normal" childhood, no violence my father didn't even swear and being an only child I was lavished with love and affection, there was always laughter to be heard when I was growing up.

I had a few relationships and then met him the man that became my abuser and tormentor for the next five years.

It all started off peachy he was very attentive, always holding my hand and giving me hugs. He told me I was "his girl" and that no matter what he would protect me. Every time there was a story on the news about a murder or accident he would hold me close and say "don't worry babe you are safe with me."

The thing was I wasn't safe and this was my initiation into a relationship that became very controlling and violent very quickly.

I called the cops the first time he struck me, a smack to the face that knocked my front tooth out, they arrested him, carted him off but he was back the next day and so the cycle continued. He'd hit me, I'd call the cops, they would get rid of him for a while but then he would be back.

The abuse got worse the violence out of control and I ended up in the emergency room so many times but I knew I had to keep my mouth shut about how I got my injuries. The stitches I had to have on the top of my legs were the worst, the lies I had to tell to cover everything up I will regret til the day I die but I was afraid. I was his punch bag, he would cut me whenever he felt like it and the rapes well there were too many.

My family and friends didn't want to know me, I was known as a liar because they all wanted to help me but I covered it up FOR HIM! FOR PEACE!

I eventually ran away in just the clothes I had on and the small amount of cash I could gather I lived on the streets for a while but was taken in and again taken advantage off, I was put back on to the streets and I had to earn money somehow so I sold myself to anyone that was willing to give me enough dollars so I could live. I got into drink and drugs, anything to numb the pain.

I am now 39 years old and I am in a healthy, loving relationship. It's took me a while but I'm getting there. I have trust issues and suffer from PTSD and I hate my scars but after speaking to Eve I have started to move on and let my past go. I would like National Coalition Against Domestic Violence to receive my share of the profits please from this book, they helped me so much.

Thank you for including my story in your book I hope it helps others because no one should have to suffer.

Tanya

Message from Eve – Brave, brave lady you have endured so much and thank you for allowing me to be your friend. We have shared our journeys together and I know I have gathered great strength from talking to you and I hope you feel the same. We may have the "pond" separating us but please know I am here for you. Your friend in England. Eve x

CHAPTER NINE

Katie's story

My story starts when I was a twenty-four year old divorced, single mum and a chance meeting with a neighbour's friend. I first saw "David" when I nipped round to get some advice on some decorating I was doing and after chatting for a while my initial thoughts and feelings were "what a lovely guy." As time passed we began to see more and more of each other, David spent a lot of time playing and building a relationship with my son who was three years old. David made me feel special he would say lovely things to me and buy me the odd gift from time to time, I was what people would described as a confident, chatty outgoing person who very much wore their heart on their sleeve.

Within a couple of months I was smitten and David moved in so we could become a proper family. At first everything was just perfect we would go to the local park and feed the ducks or take a day trip to the seaside and do all the other things a family did. When I first met David I was a full time mum and devoted my life to raising my son but after being together for over a year I felt I needed something more in my life so I decided to visit my local college to see what courses were available. I found a course I liked the sound of and I enrolled there and then and started in the September, however by the November things at home started to crumble.

At first it would be questions, for example "who had I been talking to at college?" As I felt I had nothing to hide I mentioned who I had been chatting to, one of whom was a man called Sam. At that point I felt as if a switch had been flicked and David's attitude changed – from that day my life changed forever. I will never forget the look in David's eyes they just "glazed over and within seconds I found myself thrown on to the couch and told never to speak to Sam again. I sat there dazed and confused for some time.

After this incident I was hit with a barrage of mental abuse, at first it was the odd comment here and there until in the end it became a daily mantra for David. He would say things… "You are fat and nobody will want you", "You are a wanna be and you will end up a nobody". These words haunted me for a very long time and only made me feel worse as due to the fact I am dyslexic I was finding my college course hard going. David had found a weakness and continued to chip away at it this resulted in me not being my usual chatty, bubbly self, my confidence began to disappear, myself esteem was at an all-time low and worst of all I started to believe what he was saying. On the odd occasion when we went to see family and friends I was always walking on egg shells, if I ever said anything that annoyed David I would be given one of those looks that I knew meant "wait till we get home!"

The physical abuse became worse I would be pushed against a chair or a wall with David's hand squeezing my jaw line which was just centimetres away from my throat. I would freeze with fear and see that all so familiar glazed look in his eyes.

David would often tease me or play mind games, for example he would hide my mobile phone charger in the hope my phone would run out of charge thus limiting my communication with the outside world. Before I knew it I was making excuses to not see friends and soon they fell by the wayside, it was easier to make the excuses than face the torrent of abuse I would have received if I had gone, my world was closing in and I began to feel like a caged animal.

After three years of abuse I had become worn out and I knew it would only be a matter of time before something serious would happen, I had become so low and withdrawn that at the time I was unaware I was suffering with severe depression. One of the big wakeup calls I had was when an argument erupted, I managed to get my son and run to the car and before I knew it I was driving to the local beach (to this day I always say to people if I am very stressed you will find me walking on the beach in bare feet – I find something very calming and grounding in doing this). However, while driving down the motorway that day I had thoughts of just wanting the nightmare to end, my following thought was; "the road is clear, if I drive the car as fast as I can I could turn the car into the central reservation and the nightmare would end. In that split second I looked down and saw my son sat in the passenger's seat and it was at that point something inside me changed I just knew I could not go through with it. The truth is if it had not been for my son I really don't know if I would have been here today.

The second wakeup call happened when an argument broke out in the kitchen, David had become enraged about the fact I was late in from college and was accusing me of seeing someone else and this escalated to both physical and mental abuse. David had me held against a wall with his face inches from mine shouting and pointing at me, when he let go of me I grabbed the nearest thing to me which was a plastic sugar canister and threw it against the back door. It shattered and there was sugar everywhere, I just covered my head with my hands and slunk down the kitchen cupboards and cried. I was waiting for the reign of blows to come down on me, but instead David threw a dustpan and brush at me and told me "to clean the mess up now!" That night I laid in bed with tears silently falling from my eyes suddenly I had a thought about what had happened in the kitchen that day and I asked myself "if there had been a knife on the side, would I have picked it up?" I am not ashamed to admit I probably would have picked it up. That thought frightened me and at the same time made me realise the stark reality that one of us could have ended up in prison or worse dead and who would have looked after my son then? However I was still living in fear every day.

The final straw came a couple of weeks later, when I was due to visit my mum. David had hidden mine and my sons flight tickets, as the days where drawing closer to leaving I became more and more worried that he would not hand over the tickets, again I was being teased and mentally abused. With a few days to go I knew I had to get them from him, so I tried to pick my moment carefully. David had asked me to make him a cup of tea so I jumped up immediately and made him his usual milky tea, as I handed it to him I sat down across the room and with beating heart I calmly asked him for the tickets. He responded by saying "you won't need them as you won't be going." Something inside me snapped and I told him "I am going and you won't stop me!" The next thing I knew David was on his feet shouting at me, everything happened so quick, I saw him throwing his tea at me, I managed to move my face so it hit my top. I could feel the heat over my chest, I was lucky I was wearing a thick sports sweatshirt and thankfully there was no lasting damage done. At that moment I picked up the phone and dialled 999 and within fifteen minutes the police where at my house. As they parked up they could see David shouting and pointing at me through the lounge window. David was restrained very quickly and removed from my property, I arranged a time when he could collect his belongings.

Slowly I breathed a sigh of relief as I felt that this would be the end of the nightmare, how very wrong and naïve I was. A couple of weeks later Sam was driving my car as I had pulled a muscle in my leg and needed to go shopping. All of a sudden while driving down the road a red car came speeding towards us on our side of the road, as it got closer all I could see was those glazed eyes and anger etched on David's face, he was playing a game of "chicken." Once again I was frozen with fear and as he got closer I remember thinking "he is going to do it; he is going to hit us head on." I put my head down, closed my eyes and braced myself for the impact, but it never came. Slowly I opened my eyes to see the car had disappeared, Sam told me David had swerved at the last second, I sat there shaking and crying. Within moments the red car was at the side of us driving on the wrong side of the road and was trying to push us over in to parked cars, again something inside snapped, I became angry and lent forward and signalled for David to pull over, at that he put his foot on the accelerator and sped past us.

The road to recovery was a hard, painful and at times felt like a never ending journey. After being nearly run off the road, the local council re housed us in a different location for our own safety. For a very long time after I suffered with either sleepless nights where I would wake with every loud sound or nightmares, panic attacks – I would not go to the local town for the fear of bumping in to David.

The start of the rest of my life came about while studying at college, I was introduced to counselling. I was well aware that I needed counselling in order to move on in my life, so I took the brave step forward and was referred by my G.P. Six weeks later I was at the start of my journey of rediscovering myself. It was a long, slow, emotional, scary and at times a very painful process to go through. Please note readers who are reading this and feel maybe this is the path for them please DO NOT be put off by the above, for me personally I can say with hand on heart it was the best thing I did, I was fully supported by my counsellor to enable me to work through my issues thus freeing me from the past hurt. Since then I have become a counsellor myself I gained a BSc (hons) in counselling and complementary medicine 2:1 and more recently I have completed my advanced diploma in counselling. Over the past few years I have been working voluntary at a local well women clinic, I have to say the sad part and the true reality of my job is seeing the amount of clients who have suffered some form of abuse, too many.

I would like to take this opportunity to say to anyone who is living with any form of abuse or domestic violence, you are NOT alone, there are people and agencies out there who can and will help and support you and I wish you all the very best on your journey of self-discovery. I have found in having a voice and speaking out it to be both empowering and therapeutic and it has enabled me to have closure. I would like to finish by saying thank you to all the people who have supported me through my journey; my counsellor, G.P., tutors, friends and family, my son, my little big sister and a special message to my mumsy "thank you for always being there and I love you too the moon and back.

A big thank you goes to Eve Thomas, for providing me with an opportunity to tell my story and to reach out to others.

I give permission for Eve Thomas to use my story and my chosen charity is T.O.M. (together on a mission) a charity based in the north west of the U.K. who deal with victims of suicide and those who feel suicidal.

Katie

Message from Eve – Well done you! Katie you are so brave and have been through so much and yet still managed to educate yourself so you can help others, I admire you so much. There is life after domestic violence and I am so happy that you have now found both your voice and the strength to share your story. I noticed you wrote on your status that you are proud of yourself, GO YOU SO YOU SHOULD BE! Katie went on to marry Sam and is now living her life in peace and harmony and wears a smile now instead of tears.

CHAPTER TEN

Is 50 shades abuse?

I began reading the 50 shades book as my partner bought me the first book to read whilst I was in hospital, I guess it was his way of saying sorry as to why I was in hospital! I'm not a very good reader and it took me a while to get into the book, but with nothing more to do I managed to read the first book pretty quick.

I discussed the book with my partner and said I could understand why everybody was raving on about it; at this point he too started reading the book as I started the second book. I guess the books made us both want more sex, and I was ok with that.

I never once recognised my life in the book or even registered that the wonderful Mr Grey was a perpetrator of abuse. I thought he was a nice caring, protective guy who dearly loved his girlfriend and wanted the very best for her. It was a little bit like my relationship. My partner was very protective, caring and would do anything for me. Or would he???

Here I will explain a little about my story.

After reading the books I saw something on twitter called 50 shades is abuse, at first I thought the ladies doing this account must be mad, did they know what they was talking about? Did they heck, how could they be saying such daft things? Had they even read the books? I started reading these tweets on a daily basis and following people who showed support to this account just to see what it was all about. I then followed a lady called Eve; she had website details so I decided to look at her website. By now things had started to fit together like a puzzle but the puzzle was far from completed. I had realised I was following Eve and such supporters because deep down I guessed that my relationship wasn't perfect. That the man I loved wasn't who I was making out he was. Yes he was protective like Mr Grey, that protective that if a man approached me whilst out I would be questioned and questioned as to who he was, what he wanted, was I having sex with him, how I was acting like a slag in order to attract male attention.... that sometimes led to me being taught a lesson, as he would say 'I just needed to learn'. I remember once being in a club when my cousin shouted me, we hugged as he had been away in the army and was on leave, we chatted for ages, danced and then I introduced my partner to him. All was fine until we got home to his apartment that night and we got into bed and he began to ask me 101 questions about why he had never met my cousin before. He didn't believe he was my cousin and was serving in the army and said we had both made that story up... after being called every name under the sun AGAIN he wanted to kiss and cuddle, I was mega pissed off and put my foot down saying no! That night I was made to stand at the bottom of his bed whilst he constantly insulted me for hours. He then allowed me back into his bed as long as I agreed to have sex. This is when I remember things going downhill.

I was confused as to what was happening, I knew I was hard work so I just thought and I guess I still think I deserve this treatment. I knew that when I had a drink I get a bit wild so maybe I was attracting attention and he was right to do what he did. I felt I brought shame on him so he was just teaching me to be good. As the relationship went on and more and more began to happen this just became normal, in fact I was pleased that the beating no longer hurt me physically and I was an expert at making excuses as to how I gained bruises. My friends now think I'm such a dippy girl and I'm known as being blond... this is because I make so many excuses about falling, drinking and falling.... all the original stories I guess, walking in to walls, falling down stairs... you name it I will have used it.

How was I to know that being forced to have sex when I didn't want to was classed as rape... surely you can't be raped in a relationship? I just thought I was a prude who wasn't into trying new stuff and boring, he had a high sex drive and said I was lazy!

You see E.L James, I guess my point is to me this behaviour in your book was normal to me and surely someone writing about it like you did reassured me it was perfectly normal. I mean there wasn't any inclination that this behaviour was not normal, so this confused me more and made me believe I was the one who was weird and being soft. Ana got beat and people thought this was caring as did I. Ana was made to have sex and do new things and this turned people on so I too did this. Ana was made to hide bruises so I doing the same was normal – only it was bloody hard to cover black eyes up! Ana was driven here there and everywhere, so again I not being allowed to be independent was him being protective, is this correct? BULLSHIT... the behaviour portrayed in your books led me to believe that I was the fucked up one so I stayed with my partner.

I guess though without reading your books I would never have been educated by 50 shades is abuse and the lovely lady Eve, and wouldn't have realised I'm in a relationship with a perp.

I am still very confused with things that happen and still learning things every day. I'm still in a relationship with this man and love him but I guess I'm working on how I can make a life free from being scared and being abused....50 shades of grey is about abuse, it does normalise and I am not a troll or a witch but a very scared victim of some horrendous abuse. Being with him was like being on the big dipper... The highs where amazingly good, I felt all the love in the world, he showered me with hugs, treated me to anything I wanted, made me feel special and I forgot all the things he'd done to me previously... The lows where absolutely horrible, I didn't know who I was, what was going to be coming next, I wanted to be dead, he'd go from beating me to forcing me to having sex in the space of an hour.

He had a bat that he called 'twat bat' he often threatened me with this but never used it... I used to think how lucky I was he wasn't using this on me.... How wrong was my thought process? But that was and how my mind works...

I remember being in the pub once at the very beginning and we was holding hands... I was joking with his friends and he squeezed my hard so hard I thought he'd broken my fingers.... As our relationship progressed I knew that if that ever happens whilst we was out I was due a beating when I got back with him.

He used to constantly say he'd caught a STI off me, I knew this was impossible.

He said he'd been and had a test... He wouldn't however let me go and get tested... I believed for months and months and months he'd given me a STI and I was highly embarrassed of this... Until last week when I asked the doctor to do a test and I was clear.... This was a huge relief but I was ashamed of going through the whole testing process... Mental abuse!

I got pregnant and he screamed at me for this, saying I had trapped him. Although he refused to use protection and wouldn't allow me to take contraception pills. He again wouldn't let me go to the doctors. This was the lowest point of my life. I thought I'd have to be with him forever, I thought he'd always have a hold over me. A few weeks ago he battered me that hard that I lost the baby; again I didn't go to the hospital until it was too late. I hold enormous guilt for this, I often think I wanted him to do it so I wouldn't have to make the decision of terminating and I'd be free from him. This whole situation still makes me very sad and I think about it every day.

He's drugged me on nights out 'for a laugh' and I laughed with him the morning after... Not knowing what he'd done the night before, he's held me hostage in his house in my underwear so I couldn't get out... I felt sorry for him? Really, what is that about?

At the minute I'm going through a stalking stage, I've had my car smashed up and now park streets away from my house, I've had my social media account hacked, he finds me in places I go, I guess I've put my life on hold at the minute whilst he's having the time of his life.

Money was no object to him so he'd shower me with gifts, I thought this was great but the phone he got me was tracked, He bought me a car and constantly threatened to take it off me and stated where I could and couldn't go, he bought me an iPad... But this was because he'd smashed my computer up and was able to check my history whenever he liked.

He used to drum it into my head who'd believe me and how it would make me look stupid because of the job I did. He made me paranoid about my friends to drive a wedge between us, He made me dependent on him so I wouldn't do things alone then he'd state who'd want me.

He stopped me going to the gym, he stopped me doing charity work, my days had to be timed, I worked to an itinerary, I sent over hundred texts a week the list is endless.

I've been raped, made to have sex in the weirdest places and do degrading things that will never leave my memory, jumped all over, tied up, constantly called and put down, pissed on, you name it and I've done it and all in my twenties... And I thought this was love?!

I still love this man and it worries me I will get back with him as I'm weak and depend on him.

Message from Eve - This lady is no longer a victim but a survivor and together we are working to get her independence back! She is petrified and won't go to the police but one day I hope she will be safe and at peace. Your friend Eve x

CHAPTER ELEVEN

I don't think I ever talk about how I grew up. I know I've spoken about how I was sexually abused by my stepfather and uncle and neglected by my mother. But I never really talked about the things I heard growing up. So here goes...........
Growing up was crazy for me. My parents always argued. Before I was born my mother and real father used to fight always according to what my mother told me and what my sister and brother witnessed. But after I was born my father stuck around until I was like 2 or 3. That's when my stepfather began raising me. After that my mother and him would always argue. They got physical with each other. They got to the point where my mother would get a knife and try to hurt my stepfather. I remember one time she chased him down the stairs and in order to escape from her, he jumped out the window and broke his leg. This happened when I was younger. She has had so much anger in her we didn't know where it came from. There were other times where she got angry at me and threw figurines at me. One Thanksgiving Day I wanted to spend it at my sister house, this was when I was in middle school, and my mother woke up angry. She had given me permission to stay with my sister for the four day vacation we had from school but that morning she woke up in a bad mood. I blamed myself because I knew she was in a bad mood but I kept asking her if I could stay with my sister but she changed her mind and said no. She had gotten angry and grabbed me by my hair and threw me against the floor and I hit my face on the arm of the rocking chair and I had a bruise on my face.

After that incident my mother allowed me to go to my sister's house where my real dad saw the bruise. When I went to school the following week, DCF (Department of Children and Family) came to the school to talk to me. I am not sure if it was my father who told or an aunt who was at the house that day. DCF talked to me and told me they had spoken with my mother. When I got home that day my mother had packed up my things and kicked me out. It was hard growing up listening to my mom and stepfather argue. The point that I am trying to make is that I grew up in a home where there was domestic violence involved. But yet I turned out ok. Instead of letting this affect me which in some ways it does, but I am ok. Sometimes I suffer from panic attacks. I can't deal with people yelling at me. I can't hear people yelling period but I manage to get through it. I thank God I made a promise that I wouldn't go down that road myself. Not only did I have to deal with domestic violence but also child abuse and sexual abuse. It was hard growing up around that. When people yell at me or around me, I cringe and feel like a child again. I get nervous and I shut myself away from everyone. I am afraid to say the wrong things to people because I am afraid that they will get angry and scream at me. I try so hard to fit in everywhere I go. I am not sure if those are some of the effects of domestic violence but I believe it may be.

Message from Eve – Thank you so much for sharing your story with us. Abuse takes on many forms and you have shown us that it isn't always at the hands of a man. Big hugs to you and I hope that as you continue on your path through life that you become stronger every day. Eve x

CHAPTER TWELVE

Hi Eve

I would love to be given the opportunity to share my story. I was with my husband of 9 yrs. He was a colleague at a local supermarket where we both worked the night shift. We were living together within months of meeting; he left his wife and home to be with me. He was clingy and unusual but seemed intelligent. A former heroin addict he was obsessed with suicide, punk rock & sex/porn. He weighed approximately 8 stone, tattooed, rotten teeth, scars from needle use on his arms & huge scars on his chest where he self-harmed in a similar way to Sid Vicious.

Our relationship involved us both drinking a lot of lager & listening to a lot of his music & talking into the small hours. He never helped with chores or domestic responsibilities. He bestowed me with compliments from the outset and he seemed tuned to my most intimate thoughts. He called me his 'soul mate.' I had children from previous relationships and we have 2 sons together. Now to outline some of the abuse:

I have good reason now to think that he was drugging me during the relationship (I've never used illegal substances & was very naïve of drugs & their effects although it is fair to say I liked a drink) I'd wake up after 'unexplainable' blackouts, I was always ill with chest infections, sore throats, diarrhoea, paranoia. I developed OCD, chest pain, heart palpitations etc. and my GP suspected angina & told me to watch how much I drank.

I continued to work all the same, I carried on. He was very sexually demanding, I'd wake up to find him having sex with me, he'd film me (sometimes asleep under bedclothes) I don't want to go into all of the sexual abuse but he raped me on one occasion & when I felt so low & abused afterwards he told me to cut my wrist; so I did.

I ended up with a mental health diagnosis of 'borderline personality disorder' as a result because I did not disclose the abuse to the GP or psychiatrist.

He'd never let me out of his sight, I was isolated from friends & family, he was jealous of my other kids & anyone who tried to befriend me, he didn't like any other man looking at me, made me paranoid about what I wore. He hid debts, hid porn (blaming my daughter for it), gambled, changed my name, ran up my credit cards without my knowledge whilst at the same time stashing money in the form of shares for himself. He'd tell my children that I was 'mental' & laugh at me when I got ill. I was forced to feed a family of 5(6 at weekend) on £35 a week, he said if I ever left him or cheated he'd kill me, he very nearly did!!..

He was always overly "nice" and has every personality trait of a sociopath. If I complained he'd either minimise the issue or blame me and he'd look at me with death in his eyes.

I stopped complaining but became increasingly ill. In 2010 he told me I no longer needed to take my anti-psychotic & anti-depressant meds.

I ended our relationship several months later after an incident where he groped me and punched me to the ground. He called the police telling them I'd fallen about 2 weeks later I believe he got into the house (as he still had keys), laced my food/drink with something that caused near heart failure, lungs filled with fluid, severe dehydration and approx 6 months of paranoid schizophrenic symptoms..(on research from internet I believe methamphetamine is a possibility). My teeth and hair fell out, I was so ill but the hospital never carried out a drug test!! They put me on an alcohol detox and said I'd suffered panic attacks & 'adjustment disorder' due to the breakdown of my marriage!!

He got into my home, moved stuff around, left a paranoia inducing play-list on my Ipod, left distressing items such as notes, cards & newspaper cuttings, poured corrosive over my belongings, left underwear in my drawer that wasn't mine, left strange items in the loft that I'd never seen before. He tampered with the car, left windows open, switched off the washing machine at the back, killed the goldfish, bombarded me with paranoia inducing texts and calls such as "my heart and brain are in hell, but I'll send my love even from prison, heavy breathing on the phone, stole items, turned up at my door quoting passages from the bible, turned up at my medical appointments, accused me of 'sending people after him', tried to have me sectioned, phoned me in the mental hospital laughing and taunting saying I'd never see the kids again.

I walked 30 mile out of the mental health unit to get back to my kids but the police picked me up. There was a huge carry on at the hospital because he'd changed my name, they had no record of me and thought I was totally delusional! He snatched our kids giving me no contact address.

There so much more detail I have not got down on here but I'm so damn lucky to be alive. I still fight for residency but have such little proof. I get minimal child contact and struggle to provide for the time my boys are here on the little money I receive from state welfare due to illness. My ex has not worked a day since taking the children, he claims welfare benefits and I believe he still drinks heavily and abuses drugs. My children are unkempt and not cared for properly but again I have little proof. I have sent complaints to the police, social services, hospitals and psychiatrists, who were all very sympathetic but unhelpful. I believe he wanted me dead, he'd even manipulated me into signing my will to him and I found a copy of a life insurance policy I'd never seen. My experience was like something from a Steven King movie the severe paranoia was absolutely terrifying, I felt so un-believed until I went Women's Aid. I was too scared to come out of my bedroom and use the rest of my home at first, I barricaded myself in.

Now I'm a volunteer at Women's Aid and I carry out service for my local AA group. I am abstinent from any alcohol for more than 2yrs so that hospitals will never make the mistake of misdiagnosing me again!! I still have to meet this man to collect my kids, I'm not afraid of him anymore. I am free and safe today.

Message from Eve – I really cried when I read this very courageous ladies story. I hope you are reunited with your children one day and that they are back safe with you. You have shown a great deal of bravery and I hope that you stay safe and get the proof you need. Eve x

CHAPTER THIRTEEN

My story of child abuse and domestic violence

I was 46 before I realized I had been abused. I had been abused my entire life. My first memories of childhood were of my sister "teasing" me: destroying my teddy bear, leaving me alone in town, and locking me out of my own bedroom. The only stories my family told me of when I was a baby were that I burped and farted a lot. No one remembers my first word, my first steps or anything cute I did. I was always reminded that the only reason I was even born was to keep my father from being drafted for World War II. Shouldn't that make me even more cherished? I saved his life, and yet I was still treated as an annoyance.

My father was absent most of my childhood. My mother showed me how much she hated every chance she got – which was every day. She called me lazy when I listened to the radio while doing chores, she told me that I was the worst daughter anyone's nightmares could image, and she told me that if it weren't for me she'd be happy. I think I knew some of the things she said weren't true, but it's hard to remember the truth about yourself when you hear awful things every day.

I couldn't wait to get out of her house. I went to college as far away as she would let me go. At least she didn't expect me to visit that often. I even found internships every summer so that I would never have to live with her again. My first year at school I met John. He was older, handsome and he liked me! I couldn't believe anyone would like me, especially someone as handsome as John. When I was a junior he asked me to marry him and I said yes as fast as I could.

I got pregnant with my first child while I was still in college. I had wanted to get my degree before starting a family, but this was before The Pill and John would talk me out of using my diaphragm most times. I've learned now, that that is a sign of control, but at that time I couldn't see it. I even thought he was being romantic.

After my son was born, John's controlling and manipulative ways became more obvious. I always had to have my hair and make-up perfect in public – even though I was taking care of a new-born. Our baby was never supposed to smell bad, neither was our house. I had to do 100% of the care of our son and the house while working full-time. I was frustrated about this, but I would remind myself that he was nice to me and would buy me nice things when he could. He also would stand up to my mother for me. If I didn't want to see her or call her, he would use his deep and imposing voice to tell her. I loved him for this. I thought he was my protector and that he saved me from her so I could put up with the things I didn't like about him.

I quickly got pregnant again (no birth control). John was home less and less frequently. He started gambling and drinking heavily. He lost his job and would sit home all day while I was at work and the kids were at day-care. I paid for everything and still did all the cooking, cleaning and caring for the kids. It was a miserable few years. One day while scrubbing the kitchen floor, I realized that

I'm basically a single parent. If I could do it all while taking care of an alcoholic, I could do it without him. I don't even remember the days that followed. It was all a blur of packing his things, moving them to his parents and changing the locks on the door. Most of our friends and family supported me; some were even surprised I stayed with him as long as I did. I never understood why no one said anything to me. If they could see how awful he was, why not mention it to me? Their silence made me think that it was normal or at least acceptable behaviour.

I felt guilty, ashamed and a failure for being divorced. My friends were so supportive, but I felt I had to get remarried right away. But who will marry a divorced woman with 2 kids? At my new job, I met a divorced father who seemed kind. After only 3 months of dating we were married. Again, now I know someone wanting to rush a marriage can be a sign of an abuser, but I thought it meant he really loved me.

Again, he stood up to my parents for me. And again I felt protected. But I quickly saw a lot of the same things in him that I saw in John. I had to do everything exactly as he dictated. I had to quit smoking even though he knew I was a smoker when we met and were married. For David, I couldn't wear make-up in public and he had to pick out all of my clothes – nothing that drew anyone's attention or was too attractive. As long as I did everything he wanted, exactly as he wanted, life was good. But if I ever strayed from his demands or forgot something, all hell would break loose and he would take it out on my kids – he never hit them, but he would demolish their spirits with words.

It should've been easier for me to leave David because he was so brutal to my kids, but it wasn't. It was actually harder because I didn't want to be divorced twice: a two-time loser. I convinced myself that because my kids were so young that his words weren't hurting them. After over 10 years with him I finally left when I realized he had squandered both of my kids' college savings and taken out additional mortgages on the house for his get-rich-quick schemes. He did all of this without asking me and when I confronted him about it he told me of another idea he had that would more than make up for it. This plan would require us to move across country to a state and city where we didn't know anyone. I refused to move with him. He moved by himself and somehow it made me feel better since he left me.

My mother was relentless with attacks after my second divorce. I was doing everything I could to keep my kids safe and support us and all she did was point out every mistake and misstep I took. Even though I was in my late 30s at this point, I still couldn't even hang up on her. I would listen to all of it without even defending myself. Sometimes I had enough courage to think "I don't deserve this" but I never said it out loud. She wanted me and my kids to move back in with her. This should have been a supportive suggestion, but I knew it was just another way for her to control me. I knew it would be hell on earth.

After a few lean years of struggling I met a man who had me believe he was wealthy and wanted to take care of me and my kids. He would fly the two us off to an exotic location at a moment's notice. He would buy me little gifts for no reason. He would hang up the phone for me when my mother called. He would take me to fancy restaurants and call me his princess. I thought THIS is what love should be. This is what I've been waiting for. This time, I waited an entire year to get married – I thought I had finally figured everything out.

Nope. He was just like my previous husbands. As soon as we lived together, he controlled everything. He decorated the entire house even my kids' bedrooms. He got me a new job so his friend could keep tabs on me. He controlled every penny – he would give me cash for the groceries and the check the receipt to make sure I gave him the exact amount of change. I knew a lot sooner in this relationship that it was toxic for me but I didn't know how to leave. How do I divorce three men? What is wrong with me that I made this romantic man turn into a verbal abuser? I remember telling my daughter that I wished he would just hit me. If he hit me or her, I could leave with a clean conscious. But since he only used his words, I thought that I should be able to take it. Words aren't supposed to hurt, right?

I left him after about two months of planning. It wasn't any one thing, but the day I woke up and contemplated smothering him in his sleep, I knew I had to get out. After I left him, I realized the common denominator in all these relationships was me. I joined a support group and was relieved to meet other women who had similar experiences. After many years of therapy and support, I can see how even though I hated being verbally abused, it was familiar to me. It was all I knew from childhood and all I thought I deserved. So even unconsciously, I was drawn and attracted to abusive men.

I decided to stop dating after my third divorce. There's still too much pain and shame that I'm trying to deal with. I never resolved my anger towards my mother before she died. I wish I had. Now that she's gone, I see that my strong desire to "honor" my mother and father left me unable to confront her or even really feel anger toward her. I've started meditating which is really helping me be okay with my feelings.

I want every woman to know that she is a whole and complete person without a relationship. I want every person to know that you have to honor yourself before you honor your parents or spouse. I'd also like to tell everyone to listen to their instincts more. If you feel like someone is bad news, listen to it. It doesn't have to make sense, just listen. Your head is capable to talking you into crazy situations that your instincts won't. Finally, I want everyone to know that you can feel better. It's taken me almost 20 years, but I like myself now. I never could've said that before.

Message from Eve – A lot of respect coming your way and a very big hug. Eve x

CHAPTER FOURTEEN

Hi Eve

I have been following you on twitter and wanted to know if you could include my story in the new book of survivor's stories. You said that writing helped you as you became a survivor so I'm hoping it helps me too.

I have been a survivor for almost 4 years now but I was with my violent husband for 10 years before that.

My parents died when I was small and my grandparents raised me as best as they could. Both of them had health problems and money was tight but they lavished me with love and I had a really good childhood. At 18 I left home to go to university and although it was scary I knew that my life was just beginning.

I met Joe in my third year at university, I was doing a law degree and I fell in love almost instantly. We were never apart and when I finished university he moved back home with me to my grandparents. They loved him and my Nan would always say that we looked very much in love.

Eventually we got our own house and we settled into our new lives, I loved my job and worked hard to get a promotion Joe always spurning me on, supporting me. My grandparents passed away and Joe was there by my side, holding me close whilst I sobbed uncontrollably.

When I was almost 31 I feel pregnant by accident, I was on the contraceptive pill, my career far too important to waste nine months carrying a baby not to mention the years looking after a child. Joe was happy at first but as the weeks past I noticed his moods changing and he would often have a pop at me for no reason. I was fighting my own demons, half of me was happy to be having a baby the other half mourning the loss of my career.

I was 22 weeks pregnant when Joe attacked me, his fist smacking me hard in the face. I remember being shocked but afterwards when I was alone (Joe stormed out of the house after he hit me) I began to think about our relationship in depth. Although he had never hit me before he had controlled me and emotionally abused me.

I was distraught! I am an intelligent woman why didn't I see it?

Joe came home that night and apologised, we talked and he promised he would never do it again and blamed stress.

Four weeks later I ended up in the hospital losing our baby after he beat me so badly that I ended up haemorrhaging.

As I lay mourning the loss of my child I knew what I had to do. My face was battered, my arm broken, my baby dead, I asked the nurse to call the police.

Joe was arrested, I gave evidence and he is now serving a long prison sentence. I am slowly trying to recover. I've gone back to work but I don't ever think I will be the same person again.

I feel so lonely; I've lost my parents, my grandparents, my man and my baby. I'm in counselling and it helps but Eve you were correct, writing this story has helped me so much and I want to say a really big thank you to you, now I feel as if I have some closure, my demons have been cast away and I'm ready to start living again. Thank you, God bless you.

Message from Eve – I am so happy that you reached out and I'm glad I have been able to help you. I am by no means a professional but I am a professional survivor. Thank you for sharing your story with us, I hope that it has given you closure but remember don't be alone reach out there is always someone there for you. Your friend, Eve x

CHAPTER FIFTEEN

I was 19. I was a first year student at University. I only wanted a job to make some extra pennies whilst studying, so I took a second job as casual bar staff at a local events venue. Little did I know that doing this would change my life quite so much.

He was 25 and a local boy. He had that bad boy air about him and was very confident. I think it was only my second shift when I got placed on a bar with him, I was still not very confident at the job and he seemed to know that. I found myself doing hardly anything as he effortlessly worked the bar. The only way I can describe him is he was like a shark and I was the prey, he was going to stop at nothing to charm me into a date with him. The funny thing is my gut instinct told me he wasn't a good person and to stay away, but I wasn't confident enough to trust myself.

Before I knew it I had agreed to a date, this guy was smooth he knew all the right things to say he couldn't keep his eyes off me, he made me feel so special, referring to me as his 'princess' and 'babe'. I thought I had found Mr Perfect, a bit of a bad boy but a caring loving boyfriend. By the end of a few drinks that is exactly what he labelled us boyfriend and girlfriend. I felt so flattered I completely ignored the speed at which this guy was working. That same night he even managed to persuade me to let him stay the night. The next morning he convinced me to have sex with him by bombarding me with compliments and that he simply couldn't wait. I told him I wanted to wait, but he got his way, it would be the first of many occasions where my rights and feelings were to be trampled all over. There were so many warning signs just in that first meeting, if only I knew them back then.

He appeared to be completely smitten. He would always walk me to work, meet me for lunch, and then pick me up from work. Throughout the day I would get a flurry of texts and calls too. We seemed to spend every moment together. He had virtually moved himself in after a week or so I was quickly introduced to his grandmother and was soon a regular visitor at his insistence. He spoke of grand plans to book a holiday to Mexico, by the end of two weeks he declared his love for me that he would die for me and he couldn't live without me. I was well and truly hooked in by the romance.

I had rarely seen any of my friends or housemates since I had met him, he would say I was neglecting him, or I didn't really love him, why would I want to go out I had a boyfriend now? I didn't need to go on the pull, why couldn't he come too? He would say he didn't want to loose me that he was jealous and insecure, so I would always give in and end up staying with him. He was gradually cutting me off from all my support networks and I didn't notice.

One summer evening we were getting ready to go out, I had some washing to collect from the launderette; I told him I was just popping across campus to get it. Whilst I was there I bumped into a guy on my course and we started to chat, which meant of course I didn't return quick enough for his liking. I looked down at my phone to see I was being bombarded with texts and calls to ask where I was. I turned around and out the window I could see him red faced and angry storming towards the launderette. I grabbed my clothes and ran out I took a different way back to my room to avoid him and buy myself some time, I felt absolutely petrified, I had done nothing wrong. A blazing row ensued, I didn't love him, I ruined the evening, he was insecure every excuse and accusation was thrown at me. Suddenly he was quiet and just started kissing me. Before I knew it we were having sex, I didn't want to I felt angry and upset but felt I had to go along with it to pacify him. There would be many incidents to come where he would use blackmail, guilt or anger to pressure me into sex.

After the end of my first year I had to move out of halls and into temporary accommodation so I could keep my job over the summer and of course he moved in too although he promised he would find his own place soon. I began to feel suffocated by him he never left my side, he knew passwords to all my stuff and knew my pin codes to my cards, but I was made to feel that if I loved him and trusted him then this was ok. It was at this place I remember I was first physically. I had managed to somehow attend a work BBQ without him and when he found out there was hell to pay. He demanded I come back now or he will come down there and pick me up and smash up the place and punch one of male friends who supposedly fancied me even though he was gay. He seemed so angry I couldn't risk it I left the party without even saying goodbye. I got home to him drunk, I noticed it was ok for him to have a life without me, but I wasn't allowed one without him. A blazing row ensued all I remember was trying to stand up for myself and I got the hardest smack across my face. I was in shock, how could he do this me, I was meant to be the love of his life. There was a silence before I was given the reasons why he had just attacked me for wanting to be out with my friends. The list was endless and it was all accompanied by tears; he was psychotic, he was depressed, he had never got over the death of his grandfather; this excuse was to be his favourite and used over and over again! He threatened to kill himself, he took a knife from the kitchen and held it up to his stomach before he collapsed in a heap of tears, anyone would have thought I had just smacked him in the face not the other way around! He promised me he would change, that he loved me and he could only do it with my help. Me being the kind natured person forgave him and promised to help him with his various issues, even though I had always said to myself if a man ever raised a finger to me I would be gone. I soon learnt it wasn't as black and white as that. This of course was followed by the obligatory make up sex. The next day the old him magically appeared! We went on a massive shopping spree, which was all paid for with cheques from my student account, we even came home with a hamster. A massive bunch of flowers was even delivered to work, how perfect he looked to the outside world!

There were lots of physical attacks in this house to try to keep me under control arguments would break out because the rent didn't get paid and he hated my friends, one time I asked to go out and he flew off the handle and smacked me in the nose so hard it bled, of course I couldn't go out like this. I screamed that I hate him and wanted to leave he physically held me and bruised my arms as I stood there crying begging him to let me go. When I got into the bathroom there was a variety of painkillers I told him I was taking them to get away from him as I hated him for so much for what he had done. I didn't want to die I just wanted to take enough so I could go to hospital and be kept safe from him. He forced them from my hands so I couldn't do it. Its only looking back now I can see how frightening and upsetting that sounds, we had only been together a couple of months and he made me feel like that.

The financial abuse was gradually setting in. I never had enough to pay the rent he was always in and out of work. I don't think I ever had so many eviction notices as when I was with him. He took out a lot of mobile phone contracts in my name, so when the bill wasn't paid they came after me and it was my credit report that took the beating. He maxed out my credit card in one weekend mainly on booze and fags; he promised to pay me back and never did. He convinced me to open another student account, I don't know how but I ended up with three accounts all with massive overdrafts. I even got a CCJ to my name, one day I added it up I had around £10,000 worth of debt on my head. Further down the line he also managed to convince me to commit benefit fraud, this is something I'm deeply ashamed off but we eventually got caught and had to pay that back too, we were even stealing from the tills at work, I couldn't believe how low my life had sunk that I had to steal from others to pay for food and rent because he couldn't keep a job. The financial abuse was the one thing that really crippled me it took a long time to pay it back and I had to do it all by myself, I had fear of the postman for many years and I could never answer my phone through fear of debt collectors. It was only on leaving the relationship I understood that financial abuse is common in domestic abuse.

After three months together I found myself engaged! This was not an exciting time you understand, I found myself agreeing to more and more of what he wanted just to keep the peace. I wasn't ready and it wasn't what I wanted but I knew if I said no it would cause more problems. Instead of being proud and happy I found myself ashamed and embarrassed removing the ring at every opportunity. Everything felt such a mess I didn't know what to do.

After the summer I had to move again and you can guess who also shared the room with me too, yep he was right by my side! At this house the physical abuse really became a regular feature. His control on my life was increasing every day. He brought us matching football tops even though I didn't support the local team, the worst bit was he put our names on the back, but we had to swap. This meant he forced me to walk around with a top I didn't like with his name on the back, how's that for stamping your ownership on your property?

Violence would occur any time I tried to stand up for myself or challenge him that's when an attack would take place. Usually this would be because I wanted to go out with friends this would always cause an argument. He would physically restrain me to the point where you could see finger print marks on the top of my arms. He would throw me onto the bed and spit on my face it felt so degrading, I suffered nose bleeds, black eyes he even told his boss he done it play fighting! The worst attack I can remember was when he tried to strangle me he then threatened to rape me but spat in my face and said I wasn't worth it. He tried to smother me with a pillow I really thought I was going to die so I kicked him in the nuts, grabbed by phone and ran out the door screaming. I just ran and ran tears were running down my face I was lost round some back roads I had no idea where I was but I knew I had to keep running as he would find me. My housemate rang me she had heard the commotion asking me what was happening I was just screaming, trying to run as fast as I could, no idea where I was going, I never thought of calling the police, nor did anyone else. I never remember how I ended up back at the house or how this incident ended, but we both ended up back together and the incident swept under the carpet. I'm sure he would have spent the next few days on his best behaviour.

He continued to abuse me sexually, often using sex to diffuse an argument and to make up, he would often use it as a bargaining tool. For example he would say if he had been good, as in not violent, or nice to me he would demand anal sex or oral sex, saying I didn't love him if I didn't do it. One time he forced anal sex and it hurt so much he actually cut me inside. He started to control my body too, saying I should shave all my pubic hair, that I should get a belly button piercing, dye my hair red, grow my hair pit hair, the list was endless as to what I should do to look more attractive to him. He would tell me he had a high sex drive and needed satisfaction at least 3 times a day. I would find myself being touched up in the night whilst I was trying to sleep. He would often make me watch porn with him and then re-enact it, he would buy costumes and tell me I had to dress up. One of his favourite role plays was to act like a stranger and play out a rape I was mentally and physically exhausted. I still did not recognise that what was happening was domestic abuse. This would not happen for another 2 years.

So much had happened in only six months, but the biggest shock was to discover I was pregnant. I remember just sobbing, this was not what I wanted, nor was I ready I had only just started my second year at University. He just laughed, like he had accomplished some sort of sick mission. I felt like my life was over and from this point on I was to be told I was used goods, and nobody would want me now, the violence also continued, including him punching me in the stomach repeatedly, denying he was the baby's father. I became totally dependent on him I didn't know which way to turn, I walked out of my job I had become so unreliable as he would often phone me in sick after an argument, my colleagues really resented me. This is of course what he wanted I was so dependent on him I had lost all my confidence and actually felt like I couldn't cope on my own.

Just before my daughter was born we moved yet again this time no housemates so I was stuck with him all alone, this was going to be a fresh start he promised. We wouldn't have problems anymore because we would finally be alone in peace, without people interfering. The number of physical assaults in this place was a lot lower; this is because now he didn't need to use violence so much to control me. I knew if I didn't ask to go out he wouldn't kick off, thus no argument and no beating. The only attack I can remember is when he pushed me into a wall when I was holding our newborn daughter in my arms, he would keep me in line with mental abuse mainly name calling telling me I was fat now and nobody would want me.

I continued my final year at University we would be on the move again before I graduated, back to my hometown. This would be our last home together. In this place he would constantly remind me how good he had been and stopped hitting me. I know now this is because he was always in control of his actions and could stop at anytime but chose to be violent. Also I knew the rules of the game by then and what I should and should not do to keep him on side. He seemed to favour banging and slamming objects as a warning and I would quickly pacify him now we had our daughter I wanted to protect her as much as possible. He was never good at dealing with the finances; the rent on this place never got paid either the landlord had been taking form the deposit to pay rent arrears. One day though this ran out and my mum received a phone call demanding she pay the rent as she was the guarantor. This was to be the beginning of the end. My mum had never known the extent of our financial problems until now and she was furious this had happened, we were to be evicted she said she would take me and my daughter in but not him. She also asked if I wanted to be with him anymore, she could see I was not happy, I said no. From this point we were officially separated.

The next month seemed be a bit of a blur. I remember moving home and being constantly harassed by him to see him and he demanded he had rights to see our daughter. I still felt intimidated by him and scared of his threats to show my family intimate pictures and videos he had taken of me and to even tell the police I had abused him!

I did let him come over a few times every time he would spend about 2 minutes with our daughter then spend the rest of the time trying to blackmail into sex. He even rented a room in a road just opposite our house, I still felt like I was being watched and threatened by this man. I still did not understand what was happening to me, this didn't happen until he was arrested. He had spent most of his life running from the police he was wanted for a lot of things; in our time together he was arrested about 4 times normally for non payment of fines and not doing his community service. This time the courts were fed up and decided to send him to prison. At first I felt sorry for him and was really worried about him I even took his phone calls and collected some belongings. My mum found them in my room and was furious saying why was I still seeing this guy and helping him, she managed to speak to his probation officer and told my mum that it sounded like I had been abused by him and could I go in to speak with her and also I should bring back his belongings. Speaking to her completely opened my eyes, she gave me lots of information about abuse and how the cycle of abuse works. She gave me numbers of a local charity and suggested I get an injunction.

The next few months were not easy on his release he would still try to pester me I had to change passwords on my Facebook and email accounts as he had been reading them, I also changed my number. It took me a long time to not be scared of him anymore and when he threatened and demanded to see his daughter I would simply remind him of the injunction and the power of arrest, it also stated any contact with my daughter must be discussed through a solicitor. He could see I was getting stronger and no longer intimidated by his threats.

He eventually moved back to the coast and had relationships with various women, all attempts to contact me eventually tailed off. Now he had a new lady he did not need to assert power and control over me.

It was not an easy journey I suffered from depression after the split and struggled to understand why it happened to me. My self-esteem was very low, I started sleeping around to try and feel loved again and to feel special it was a big mistake. It was only after receiving phone counselling, doing the freedom programme and talking to other survivor's things started to fall into place. I was able to get control back of my life! I took up new hobbies, started going out with friends again as well as making new ones, I was able to cut my hair and get my nails done, and I was able to get clothes that I wanted! I was able to rediscover me the freedom was amazing, no one criticising me or trying to change my opinion. I learnt some very important lessons and how to listen to my instincts so I never get with another abusive man again. I have also promised myself to educate my daughter as teaching her about healthy relationships and warning signs is one of the greatest gifts I can pass on to her. Writing has helped my loads at first my councillor said it would help diffuse my anger and it did, now getting the chance to tell my story has been very liberating, if only one person reads this and feels like they can relate to it and make a decision to leave then I'm one happy lady! I did it and I never thought I could survive you can do it too. I am a survivor not a victim.

Message from Eve – This story is very sad but also so inspiring and shows just how easy it is to fall under the spell and not recognise the abuse. I applaud you and I am so happy that writing your story from the heart has helped you. Writing helped me so much over the years and the idea for this book came from wanting to help others as they journeyed from victim to survivor. This story has great detail and information and I am reaching out to every woman in the world, can you see the signs of abuse? Do you recognise any of the signs? Like the author of this chapter I too hope that perhaps if only one woman reads this book, recognises the abuse, the tell-tale signs and gathers the strength knowing that others have done it too walks away from a violent relationship then this book was worth every penny YOU spent in buying it. Much respect to the author of this chapter for highlighting abuse this way. Eve x

CHAPTER SIXTEEN

I don't really know where to start this and it will probably end up a jumbled mess because that's how my brain still feels.

I met my abuser five years ago whilst on a night out with my girlfriends, I was a bit wild back then but looking back I can now see that Mark brought me "back into line" very quickly.

I had been divorced for a couple of years after my marriage fell apart when my husband had an affair, he broke my heart and I really didn't think I would ever find anyone to love me after that. I was forty years old with 2 teenage kids, a bit on the heavy side (I over ate when I was going through my divorce) and very lonely. I wanted someone to hold me again, be there for me and so when Mark entered my life it was only a matter of weeks before we were living together.

He was handsome, funny and had my boys onside within the first month or so, I remember one day we were all at the beach and I was sat watching Mark and the boys playing cricket with the biggest smile ever on my face, I was so happy and even though Mark was a bit controlling it didn't matter I needed him to control my sometimes impulsive and childish behaviour.

He'd told me often enough that a woman of my age and size shouldn't be wearing short skirts and going out on the town, that I was "asking for it" and I'm sad to say that my boys agreed with him. I did as I was told and Mark even took me shopping to buy a new wardrobe but I hated the new clothes, they swamped me and made me look even fatter than I was.

I decided to join a slimming club against Mark's wishes (when he was in a good mood he would tell me I didn't need to slim that I was just perfect!) but that didn't last long as he cancelled the payments from my bank and told me that I wasted money and so in future he would keep hold of my cards and sort out the finances. This is when I began to think something wasn't right but by then it was too late.

I was given just the bare minimum every week to get the groceries etc but even this stopped with Mark taking control of literally everything. I was a hermit in my own home and found sanctuary in food and so the weight piled on even more.

Mark and my boys took great delight in laughing at me and putting me down constantly, my answer to eat even more.

Before I knew it I was huge and my health was suffering. To walk up the stairs caused pain and my breathing; well I sounded like a 3 pack a day smoker!

There was physical stuff too, Mark would throw things at me, call me lazy and grab me by the back of the neck whilst forcing me to look at myself in the mirror. I hated myself, I hated my life.

I had a few trips to the emergency room with broken bones and cuts oh and a burn as well where he threw a pan of hot water at me because I hadn't put any salt in the vegetables. I still have an ugly scar on my chest.

I stood it for 5 years, my boys turned against me and called me names all the time but I knew it was Mark's influence my boys were good boys.

The last time Mark beat me he did a really good job and refused to take me to the hospital but the next day I knew I needed urgent medical help.

With a smashed in face I sat in the emergency room again and had to endure the stares from the people around me, I was so embarrassed and it was then that I made the decision that changed the rest of my life, I wasn't putting up with it anymore!

I asked the nurse to call the cops and gave a statement, Mark was arrested and I gave evidence against him.

I am now 55 years old; I've lost a lot of weight and am now a size 8. I had my long hair cut short and this time I BOUGHT MY CLOTHES! My boys have said sorry many times and I have forgiven their cruelty knowing that none of this was their fault. I'm slowly getting my life back on track and have enrolled to do some night courses with the help of my counsellor, I would love to work with children who have been abused but one thing I do know is that I won't let abuse beat me!

I would like to thank Eve for all her help, you along with my counsellor have helped me so much, you are a friend and writing and sharing my story has been such great therapy. I would like my nomination to go to Ark Of Hope if that is ok.

Message from Eve – See I knew you could do it and I am so glad that writing has helped you too. Ark Of Hope it is. Your friend. Eve x

CHAPTER SEVENTEEN

This is where the old life ends and the new one begins. But first I will tell you of how mine and my children's trust were betrayed by the hands of a monster.

Now matter how hard I try to forget, I can't get the images of my children's faces of when our perpetrator struck.

It wasn't just the fact I could never do things right in every day life, it was the actions that followed. If dinner wasn't cooked right, the plate used to hit the ceiling. When the children cried, if the house wasn't spotless, if his tea was too strong, what I wore was never right. Each time I left the house, I was timed, till receipts checked, sometimes I wasn't allowed out. I was made to watch porn, he raped me, he hit me, he buggered me, he tied me up, if I refused, I'd get slapped, or raped, or both. He killed our puppy once cos things weren't going his way, that was my fault too. In fact every thing in our relationship was my fault.

I'd make him do it, he said, then without a word of warning, he'd break down, say sorry, he will change. But he never did, in fact he got worse. I was like a possession to him. To do with what he wanted, when he wanted. The sex acts he carried out, I knew weren't normal. I mean, you don't get a dog to lick to your fanny do you?!

He isolated me away from my family and friends; I had no one to turn too for help. He threatened me lots of times with a knife, and twice even a gun, just to make sure he put enough fear into me that I wouldn't leave. Then the threats to kill my family if I left him, the emotional blackmail was awful on many occasions.

The children witnessed a lot of this, but mainly the slapping, of the head being banged on the kitchen side, or me being held up against the wall, with my head banging into it.

The children suffered too, with threats of violence, with him hitting them, shaking them, and to this day, unaccountable actions. With what I know already, it is highly likely that he sexually abused the children. They refuse to talk about him. They refuse to talk about the past. All my 4 kids have been traumatised by his actions. That was back in 2001 when we all managed to escape.

The police helped me, along with the council, I went into a refuge for 4 months, yes he tried to hunt me down, he threatened my parents who are elderly, he even threatened his solicitor! I had to completely cut off my friends, and start a new life. My mum has moved now to be near me. He has no idea where we live, and that is how it will remain.

My eldest two children are now sharing a flat, both with jobs, and both typical jack the lads. But it has been a long hard slog to get where they are today. My other 2 are still at home, and still having their own problems to deal with. But we are alive, we survived, we got out.

There is light at the end of the tunnel. It's just finding it.

Please include my twitter name and my email address if anyone wants any advice or just someone to talk too or wants to leave. I have also worked with domestic violence and helped many women along the way. More than happy to help.

Message from Eve: This brave lady, Aunt Cags can be reached on twitter @therealnicebrit and by email **nicebrit@gmail.com**. Hugs. Eve x

CHAPTER EIGHTEEN

"I was severely depressed when we first met. I was also in a relationship with someone else but he was just like me – depressed and mentally ill. He would look after me in college when I had panic attacks. He understood me in a way that my boyfriend just couldn't, and I started to fall for him. It was for these reasons that I eventually left my boyfriend for him.

But in the early days it became apparent that he was more than just depressed. At times he would stare off into space and become unresponsive, at first I thought he was having an absence seizure, but then he started to move during them.

Eventually the "just moving" turned into violence. We were at my flat, alone, and he reached for my throat and started to choke me. Eventually he came around, begging for forgiveness and telling me he couldn't remember a thing. I was scared – terrified – but I wanted to be there for him through his problems the way he was there for me.

At first I thought he was possessed. When he started talking during his trances he would go by different names, and tell stories from the 1800s, as if there was a ghost trapped inside his body. But eventually it became evident that he was suffering from Dissociative Identity Disorder. I found it fascinating, and he started to seek help. The attacks continued. There was one particular alter who just seemed to want me dead. It seemed like every time we were alone, this alter would come out and try to choke me to death, and he had me on the borderline of unconsciousness more times than I could count. Though it's true what they say –

when you're in grave danger, you gain super human strength! I overpowered a man twice my size many times, and possibly saved my life.

It wasn't just me the alters had it out for, however. They would attack him, too. They made him punch himself in the face many times, and even stopped his breathing. This would terrify him and I would have to give him mouth-to-mouth until the alters released his breathing again. I felt like he needed me, so I put up with the attacks and stuck by his side. After a while, the whole thing seemed to quieten down. We were in an on-off relationship for nearly two years. I got to know a lot of the alters and the random attacks seemed to stop, but that didn't mean the violence stopped completely.

 As I suffer from Borderline Personality Disorder, I often go into bad moods for small and seemingly insignificant things. Whenever I'd get upset like this, I tended to shut myself off and keep to myself. This drove him crazy. At first he'd ask what was wrong, and as it became apparent that I didn't want to talk about it, he would get angrier and angrier, demanding to know what he had done to upset me. "If I've done something to upset you, I deserve to fucking know what it is I've done," he'd yell at me. I'd get scared, and shut off even more, and then when he reached the peak of his anger, he'd switch, and it would be back to the choking. I can't tell you how many times I felt his hand tightening around my throat, me crying as I fought and struggled, fearing for my very life. Every time he'd apologise, and every time, I'd forgive him. He couldn't help it, after all.

But as time went on, it became clear that something else was going on. My cats stopped coming home. When I brought them in they would cry at the door, terrified and wanting to be out. I didn't want to think it, but I started to wonder if the alters had been abusing the cats, too. When I first asked him about it, he outright denied it. But how would he know? His alters had a good communication system and I demanded that he search to try to find out if something had been going on.

Eventually he admitted that, yes, an alter had been abusing my cats when I had been asleep/out of the room. I felt sick. I reasoned that it was alright when he abused me – I understood his condition and knew that he couldn't help it – but my poor darling cats, they didn't have a clue what was going on, they just knew that he was hurting them and they had to be away from it.

I tricked that alter into thinking I wasn't around, waited until he picked up my cat, and then entered the room. The look on his face showed that he realised he had been caught out. I took the cat from him, placed him down, and then turned back, punching him in the face as hard as I could. The anger took over. I grabbed him by the throat as they had done many times to me, and pushed him against the wall. "If you touch my cats again, I will fucking kill you. Do you understand?" The alter looked terrified. He nodded and disappeared. Looking back, it probably wasn't the best idea to react violently. I was stooping to his level but I felt like I was standing up for my poor cats, who couldn't stand up for themselves.

I eventually insisted that that alter be destroyed. My boyfriend told me that one of his alters had the ability to "kill" off other alters, and although he reassured me that that alter was now too scared to come out after I'd attacked him, I wanted reassurance that this would never happen again. So he assured me that this alter had been killed off, and although the cats still rarely came home, I felt better.

As time went on, I was starting to think more and more about breaking up with my boyfriend. I couldn't bear that every time I got upset, it seemed to result in me being attacked. His logic was that, if I didn't want to be attacked, I should simply stop doing what I was doing – which was the natural way I behaved when I was upset. If I didn't want to be attacked I should simply stop being upset. That made sense, right? As much as that seemed to suggest it, I knew that it wasn't my fault. It's only natural for people to get upset, I couldn't control it. But even today, with my boyfriend who would never lay a hand on me, I still get a little scared when I get upset, because for so long, it always resulted in me getting attacked.

There was one incident when we were walking to my house after a night out. I was quiet as I was upset about something, and he started getting angrier and angrier, demanding I tell him what I was upset about. He grabbed me by the wrists, and the more I tried to pull away, the harder he held on, until I was in so much pain I tried to lash out, trying to knee him in the crotch so that I could get away. The fury in his eyes returned as he looked at me, and said "you shouldn't have done that."

I managed to pull away and started to run, tears streaming down my face. When he realised I'd got away from him; he switched back, and ran after me. I eventually stopped, sobbing, and he put his arms around me and apologised for everything. I was so terrified I had a panic attack. That night, I gave him an ultimatum. I told him to inform his alters that if he ever hurt me again, or if I ever found out he had hurt my pets again, it was over.

I gave him the ultimatum in March, and everything went well until August. We had agreed to go and do two weeks of work experience at a hotel in Austria – and a week before we were due to fly out; I started to have some concerns. I'd noticed that a lot of strange things seemed to be happening. On one incident, I came downstairs after showering and he had taken the cover off one of the sofa cushions – when I asked what had happened he told me that the cat had defecated on the sofa. Another time I came downstairs and was told that the cat had peed on the table. She never did anything like this when I was around – it was only whenever he was alone with her. I started to suspect he was abusing the cats again.

I also have two pet rats. Again I was upstairs, drying my hair after a shower, and I heard one of my rats squealing extremely loudly and constantly. I ran downstairs to find him holding the rat, and I asked him what the hell was going on. He told me that he'd been holding the rat, and had dropped him and then accidentally stood on him. I didn't believe this story, and I went back upstairs to continue drying my hair and I heard the rat squealing again. I ran downstairs, again asking what the hell he was doing, and he told me he had squeezed the rat's tail "to check if he had hurt him."

So the week before I was due to go to Austria, I started to notice these repeated incidents. I started to panic, convinced that he was still abusing my animals... But because we had agreed to go to Austria, I couldn't break up with him. I decided that I would wait until after we got back from Austria to break up with him. I dreaded having to make up an excuse to break up with him after we got back home, but as it happened, I ended up not having to do so.

It was about a week into the work experience. I had just finished a long shift and I had headed out to sit in the sun, when he asked me to help him polish some cutlery. I told him no, I had just finished a long shift and I wanted to relax. So instead he decided to go to my boss and get him to tell me to do it. I ended up begrudgingly doing it despite having finished my shift. I was in a bad mood with him after that, and the next day, I asked him to go outside and ask our boss where the icing sugar was. Despite what a fuss he had made the previous day about me refusing to do something off duty, I was told "no, I'm on my break". I was so angered by this we ended up having an argument. He eventually told me "I am sick of putting up with your shit". I replied saying, "well don't bother then." "Fine, I won't."

I assumed this meant our relationship was over. I went and hid in the laundry room and cried. He followed me, apologising and saying he didn't want to break up. I told him to leave me alone. He wouldn't. The argument got worse and he grabbed me by the wrists again. I forced him off me, grabbed the key to our room and ran up the stairs to lock myself in the room so that he couldn't get to me. He chased me up the stairs, and even though I tried to close the door, he forced his way in, swearing and telling me that, as it was his room too, I wasn't going to lock him out of it. I eventually locked myself into the bathroom, and he picked the lock from the outside, forced his way in and grabbed me by the throat, forcing me against the wall and squeezing my throat so that I couldn't breathe. I eventually fought him off. I told him that was it, our relationship was over. I went downstairs and requested to have my own separate bedroom so that I didn't have to be near him.

The rest of the holiday was awkward. Due to vulnerability I ended up begging him to spend the night in my room for most of the week. We did sleep together, too. But I told him that once we were back in England, it was over. At the airport, I said goodbye to him, and I have not seen him since.

The aftermath of his abuse was difficult to deal with. Sometimes I felt terrified at night, like he still had his hands around my throat, like I was still fighting for my life against him. I cut him out of my life completely and it took months before these "flashbacks" eventually subsided. I have since found a wonderful man who would never hurt me, and he has stuck with me as I struggled with the memories of these experiences, and he has made me feel safe once again. My ex no longer has a hold over me."

"I didn't leave him for me; I left him for my pets. When I started to suspect he was abusing them for a second time, I felt so weak that I hadn't left him the first time. I felt like one of those mothers who know their husband is abusing their children but doesn't leave him. I felt so weak but now he's gone and even though he has been gone for 7 months, my cats still don't come home. I feel so guilty. "

Message from Eve – It has taken a great deal of bravery for you to share your story and for that I thank you from the bottom of my heart. I hope that your cats return home and that you feel at peace once again. Never be alone. Eve x

CHAPTER NINETEEN

A long time ago I was a victim of domestic violence, it has haunted me and followed me around like a sinister shadow for years and I am hoping that by sharing my story at last that I can finally move on.

It began in the early 80's, I was a bit of a rebel back then with my bright pink and green punk rock hair. I met Dan at a gig and we hit it off straight away and found out that we had a lot of common interest's music being one of them.

We travelled a lot to see our favourite bands and back packed around Europe for an entire summer until it was time to come back and start my career.

We got married when I was 22 and I was so happy, he was my Mr Right, my Mr Perfect in every way but as soon as he got the ring on my finger it all changed.

It began on the honeymoon with him refusing to come near me, I didn't understand at the time and thought it was something I had done but by the end of the two weeks I was distraught and honestly thought my husband didn't love me.

The next year passed quickly and I found out I was pregnant, we were happy. I gave birth to our son and that is when the problems really started, he resented any time I spent with our boy and if he wanted something he would drag me away from him by either my hair or my arm.

Dan also began to rape me whenever he wanted (I now know it was rape) but again I kept silent and let him do what he wanted. I wanted to be loved and cuddled and when I found out I was pregnant again I was devastated, our second son was not conceived from love but from rape.

I struggled on and we found it really hard to cope financially and so with Dan's permission I found a job at the local supermarket, this is when my eyes began to open.

A young girl who I had gotten friendly with came into work one day with a black eye and told me it was her boyfriend my words tumbled out, I couldn't stop them and I told her about my own life and the abuse I was suffering. Claire went back to her boyfriend at the end of the shift and I went home to Dan feeling a little lighter because I had shared my secret.

I shouldn't have trusted Claire, she went into work the next day (it was my day off) and told everyone and when I arrived for my shift the day after I was met by stares from all the staff, I was so upset as person after person came to me trying to console me, I grabbed my coat and left.

I got the beating of my life when I told Dan I couldn't go back to the supermarket to work (I couldn't tell him why) and when I went to bed that night and he raped me I knew that was the last night I would lay beside my husband.

The next day whilst Dan was at work I packed enough things for me and my boys, got into my car and drove to the police station.

We spent the next four weeks in a refuge and I felt safe for the first time in a long time. Dan tried to look for me and the boys but the refuge made sure we were all secure. We moved into a new house in a new area and began to put our lives back together.

Two years later Dan found us and wormed his way back into our lives, yes I was totally stupid! He said he had gotten counselling and would never hit me again and so I took him back, it wasn't long before the beatings and rapes started again and I became a victim once more.

It took me another 15 years to finally escape and now I have been a survivor for almost 3 wonderful years. He turned on our boys, began to abuse them regularly and so I knew I had to get away for not only my own safety but theirs. They are now in relationships of their own and are good, kind men NOTHING like their father.

My hair hasn't been pink or green for years and when I look in the mirror I know I'm passed my sell by date but I don't care. I don't want another man I just want to be alone and happy and finally I have found that. My eldest son's wife Rebecca is due to give birth at the end of July and I cannot begin to explain what joy I feel, a new life for us all to love and protect.

Thank you for giving me my voice it feels really good and I think that those shadows may retreat now. I would like to nominate The Samaritans as my charity they have helped me so much and saved my life by just listening to me many times.

Message from Eve – RESPECT! You have endured years of abuse but finally you are in a happy and peaceful place and expecting the arrival of your grand child very soon. I hope that writing and sharing your story has given you some form of closure and please don't forget the pictures when he/she arrives. Take care and keep smiling. Eve x

CHAPTER TWENTY

Excerpts from 'Black & White - A Survivor Story by Renee Matthews.

Having left England, my place of birth for Nigeria at the tender age of five with my parents, I stayed there for 17 years, as my parents are both Nigerians. At 21, I met and fell in love with a handsome guy while we were both undergraduates. We were very happy together and he adored me. In return, I loved him dearly and I was ready to give him my all. Life was good.

At that point in time, my mum and younger sister had already gone back to London and the plan was for me to join them there after my graduation. I was happy and I looked forward to joining them. However, I dreaded the thought of leaving my boyfriend behind. Full of guilt, I was devastated and heartbroken beyond imagination. I almost choked on my words when I informed him of my intentions, but surprisingly, he took it all in his stride.

One year later, just after my graduation, I returned to England, and almost immediately, I set out looking for employment. Any job, for the sake of quick cash! In no time, I secured a job and worked my fingers to the bone doing menial jobs including cleaning toilets, in order to send money for my heartthrob to join me. He came. I was beyond ecstatic, in seventh heaven and I was whole again. Before long, we got married. Life was sweet, but only for a short while.

Soon the cracks started to appear. After he had gotten his papers (which was the leave to remain in the country indefinitely), he thought the sky was his limit and he began to display his true colours. A cycle of two-timing, late nights out, shameless lies, abuse, violence, torment, drug abuse, drunkenness and suicidal tendencies all soon came in quick staccato.

On several occasions, he returned home late, drunk, high as a kite and reeked of marijuana, wakibaki or weed. The weed stench was ever so strong I could taste it, and the smell was probably enough to conk out the whole neighbourhood. Nevertheless, I loved him very much. I pinned for him in his absence and I would sometimes wait until he came home so we could eat dinner together, no matter how late. When he would not come home, I would cry myself to sleep. Unbeknownst to me, he was busy gallivanting with his mates and other women, and he had, most likely, already filled his belly and much more.

Little did I know that I was embarking upon the lonely dreaded journey of abuse and misery. My hopes and dreams of pure marital bliss were shattered and, even through rose-tinted glasses, I began to realise that our love was one-sided. Yours truly was only just waking up to reality. I became his natural punching bag, but when the narcotics wore off, he came to his senses and frequently apologised for his misbehavior; blaming the devil, booze and wakibaki. I constantly forgave him, making up was great and I did not report his assaults to the authorities or anyone. Ultimately, it all got too much. His physical, emotional and mental abuse graduated to another level. A higher one! Therefore, I decided not to bury my head in the sand any longer nor to wallow in self-pity, but instead, snap out of whatever self-denial or self-doubt I imagined or thought I had.

On a fine sunny day, I took a stroll in the park to clear my head and to do a reality check. In the process, I asked myself a few questions, among which were: 'Does love really hurt? Is a 'black eye' truly an expression of love?' While pondering, I had an epiphany moment and every confusing thought seemed to click like puzzle pieces. I realised that although I loved him, I had to love me first and much more. I also did not have to put up with his abuse. Instantly, I reached a decision. I made up my mind that the next time he laid a finger on me; I would do something about it.

One fateful day, while undergoing one of his brutal pounding sessions, for as a karate black belter, he was a very strong man who was quick with his fists and feet. I thought I was going to die and I could do nothing, as my body was already going limp. However, after my ordeal ended, I managed to drag myself across the living room floor, and with the last of my strength, I stretched to grab the telephone and finally summoned up the courage to call the police before almost passing out. I was the colour purple. He was arrested overnight, although, I did not press charges because I still loved him. He got released the next day and returned home with his tail between his legs. He was very remorseful and almost cried me a river. Flooded with sympathy, I forgave him again. My epiphany or whatever moment I thought I had, flew out the window. He had learned his lesson, or so I thought. Things got better and I later became pregnant. That notwithstanding, he consistently went to town on me by sometimes beating me to a pulp and at some point, I thought I would lose my baby. It was indeed a miracle that I did not.

Due to all the emotional stress and physical abuse, my waters broke at 6 months; even before I was due to attend my first antenatal appointment. I was hospitalized throughout and my baby was born very prematurely at 7 months, which was exactly 13 weeks earlier than my due date.

Things got better. Our baby was fine, thank God, but as time went by, the devil in him resurfaced. I became more or less like a single parent since he was hardly ever at home, but when he was at home, the slightest argument would set him off and his anger was often explosive whether he was under the influence of narcotics or not. I was forever walking on egg shells. Things were rough and tough, but I bore it all as I had resigned my fate to the kind of wife that got slapped and stayed put. My crime? Love.

One day, while we were arguing, he lashed out and one of his blows intended for me, landed on my baby while I carried him. My son was terrified and was screaming non-stop. When I managed to console and calm him down, I called the police who notified the Social Services. He was arrested, and yet again, I foolishly refused to press charges against him. Deep down, I still loved him, I knew he loved our son too and I was certain that he would never deliberately hurt him. Stupid was my middle name. I was helplessly and hopelessly in love with being in love. My self-confidence was non-existent. Love had taken leave of my brain and senses. Can a Leopard change its spots? I would often think aloud now. He was such a violent man to the extent that he threatened to kill me and boasted about getting away with the crime. During one of our numerous arguments, he burst my left eardrum, which caused a blood clot. To this day, almost 17 years on now, I cannot answer a phone using my left ear and I regularly feel pain and hear strange eerie sounds.

After all I've been through with him, I am lucky to be alive. To the world, he was my prince charming and at home, nothing but an incredible hulk. I had very few friends, but I hid it all from them and my family. I became an introvert for he loved being the center of my Universe when he was home. I had allowed myself to be deceived into believing that he was just jealous and possessive because he loved me.

Growing up in a polygamous home in Nigeria, my dad had beaten up my mum, step-mum, my siblings, and me, countless times and I thought that was the normal way of life. Domestic Violence is not a big deal in Nigeria. It is a common occurrence and it is the norm. Due to societal expectations within the Nigerian community, home or abroad, a woman is meant to keep her house in order. She is the glue that holds her family together and should anything go wrong, it is believed to be her fault and she is to blame. This perception made me feel very ashamed and it led me to believe that I was responsible for his behaviour. I was beginning to question my sanity. Perhaps I was a failure and there was something I should have done, but hadn't. I was constantly playing the blame game in my head, thinking that I may have failed my husband somewhere down the line. I was also certain I would be blamed if my nightmarish situation ever got out, hence I decided to endure my marriage rather than enjoy it; for better or worse. Although it all happened to me in the UK, that was the main reason I did not speak out or take action until it was almost too late.

Eventually, I broke the silence and informed my family. With their encouragement, I summoned the courage to seek help. Fortunately, he made a few too many mistakes. By that time, I had reached my breaking point and decided that enough was enough, so, when I was presented with the opportunity to escape from him once and for all, I fled.

From my seemingly impossible situation, and from those darkest of days, it is incredible to think now that, with the combination of tremendous love, support, and a miraculous twist of fate in my favour, I have now been able to turn my life around.

Fortunately, I have found true love with Tom my amazing husband, and we have been extremely happy together for 15 years now. Loving a person, and having that person love you back is the most wonderful and amazing thing in the world. I am a successful Business Sales Executive, a Politician, and a member of the Women's Aid UK. Thankfully, I have now gained the strength, courage and the confidence to share my story in Book form, which also includes a self-help section.

I am Renee Matthews. I am proud to be a survivor, an over-comer and an Award-winning Author. My aim is to share my experiences, to help others turn their lives around and to break the cycle of domestic violence, which truly is an 'epidemic behind closed doors - A silent nightmare.'

For more information visit www.reneematthews.co.uk

Renee

Message from Eve – Thank you so much for sharing your story with us. You are a very brave lady and I hope you share my joy that #OneVoice has reached Nigeria.

Eve x

CHAPTER TWENTY ONE

The lifelong legacy of domestic violence. I do not like referring to my former husband as a man, I think it's an insult to men, he is violent, controlling, cruel, manipulative, sadistic, destructive, abusive-a man? NO!

With hindsight the violence started subtlety. My former husband constantly criticised my looks, he criticized the way the way I smiled, my voice, my cooking, the list is endless. The criticism increased over time, he would grab my hair, I could almost hear it ripping from the roots then drag me to a mirror and say "look at you ugly slag! I deserve better than you" - I still hate seeing my reflection to this day.

One sunny Sunday afternoon; he had aggressive all day, throwing his plate across the room because the meal was not to his standards he demanded to know if I had used the phone, to this day I don't know whether I had or not. He had been out side and was carrying a tin that that he had been polishing his car with, without warning and with full force he used the tin to hit me on the end of my nose, his punch had such an impact that I heard the bone crack and my nose bled profusely, spraying blood across the kitchen as he knocked me to the floor. He called me a slag and ordered me to clean up the mess that the blood had made.

This was the first of many violent assaults, I ended up having a 'nose job', the surgeon said it was like putting a jigsaw together, I was so weak that I had difficulties after the anaesthetic. I worked in the department and some of my colleagues didn't even recognise me. I arrived home following the nose surgery only to have to run in terror as he had another violent outburst and lifted the deep fat fryer and threw it at me, most of it missed me save for a few blisters on my arms. I ran and with herculean strength leaped over the fence of the garden at the back, sprinted past the astonished neighbour and ran barefoot in the direction of the main road, I thought that if he got in his car and came after me surely someone would stop and help me? I certainly had a few rubber neckers, I was barefoot, had a blood stained plaster cast on my nose and two huge swollen black eyes. I was only a few days post op and began to feel very weak, I stopped and sat down on a bench wondering what to do next, I had to go back, the children were there, I hoped that he would have calmed down; this was a pattern that would repeat itself many times.

Hospitals need to be more proactive when approaching suspect none accidental injuries in women, (and indeed men), a split head, a full thickness puncture wound to my chin and contusions to the brain causing blackouts and a year of 3 monthly scans and visits to a neurological consultant are just a few of the causes of my hospital visits, the full thickness puncture wound was two days old and infected because he had refused to let me leave the house, the mouth wash they gave me passed through from inside my mouth right through the little hole and trickled down my face! He stood beside me whilst I told the doctors a tall story that he had dictated to me to explain my injury! He refused to leave the room clearly worried that questions might be asked. The doctors however were very skilled and I am fortunate to have only a small scar there.

He would never allow me to take the children out with me; this he said was his insurance to stop me leaving. - He knew that I would not walk out without them. He told me the children would tell any official that they hated me and wanted to live with him. I will always feel terrible not being able to escape with them earlier but I really did not know what to do, would he really get the children? But what if he killed me? Then there would be no one there for them.

He constantly rang me at work so that he could keep a check on me but one day I broke down and confessed to the sister on the ward, she had already noticed the bruises and black eyes where I had 'hit my head on the cupboard door'. I had left him before briefly but I stupidly allowed him to persuade me to back, I knew it was the wrong choice but at that time I had very little support and nowhere to turn to, not to mention low self-esteem, I was physically and mentally weak at that stage weighing well below the recommended weight for my height. However with support from her and other friends and colleagues a plan was put into action. I would leave the ward a little early that day and if he rang then he would be told that I was on break/in theatre so as to not arouse suspicion.

My first port of call was the local police station, I still had a rather unattractive yellow tinge around my eyes from the fading bruise of yet another black eye I told the disinterested looking police officer my story, tearfully explaining that I feared for my life and wanted to leave but wanted to take the children with me. The response of the police officer was a blow to any hopes of escape, she told me to get myself out and then see a solicitor regarding custody; I trudged back to the place I was supposed to call home feeling very despondent and feeling that I was completely trapped.

I had felt emotionally drained but fortunately my friends and colleagues were a wonderful source of help and support, I had been unaware that when family or friends phoned they were always told that I was in the bath, I was never told that they had phoned. Isolating domestic violence victims is a common ploy to enable the perpetrator to gain maximum control.

Enquiries were made, a colleague's police officer husband gave advice and a local refuge contacted, I left work early to attend court for a hearing for an injunction, and following advice from an excellent solicitor the injunction was marked 'not to be delivered until confirmation that the applicant has left the matrimonial home.' The reason for this was that if for some reason my escape did not go to plan and the injunction was delivered whilst I was still at the house I knew what would happen, he would take delivery of the injunction, shut the door then give me what would probably be my final and fatal beating.

I escaped when he was at work, a police escort had been arranged to ensure the safe arrival of the children and myself at the refuge. Did you know that if you someone to phone you but instruct them to not put their (house) phone down after the call you can block the line for around 15 minutes? Whilst at work he would constantly ring to check that I was there so this phone blocking gave me a 15 minute window of opportunity to escape. I stuffed my car with children's clothes, toys and as much as I could get into black bags although I ended up arriving at the refuge with black bags and the clothes that I stood up in. The police escort had not arrived and terrified that he would leave work and return fuming at the constant engaged tone from the house phone I decided to flee there and then, we passed the police car with flashing blue lights en route although hey did catch up with us.

There feeling of relief when I woke up the next morning at the refuge was incredible, I didn't have to tiptoe round him anymore; I wouldn't have to worry that the next beating might be my final and fatal one.

I endured many court appearances after that as he constantly flouted the injunction having tracked me down at the refuge, the staff at the refuge were wonderful and moved me to the upper floor as they felt that I was at great risk describing him as a very dangerous man.

I eventually moved into a house from the refuge; however he managed to track me down, more violence. I was eventually told by an officer from the domestic violence unit that the only way they could protect me and ensure my safety was to be with me 24/7 and so I uprooted and moved to another part of the country. It was a difficult decision due to schooling etc. but well worth it for the safety of the children and I.

.I realise now that the bullying and belittling are a common factor in domestic violence, by the time he threw that first punch I had no confidence or self-respect. I was frightened to leave and frightened to stay. He told me that he would kill me if I left and that that he would get custody of the children; he claimed to have told people that I was clumsy and always falling downstairs and that he would use this to his advantage when he finally killed me.

Nearly 2 decades later I live in another part of the UK, I changed my name and my children's names. The bruises have faded away, I have a few scars but the real damage lies much deeper. I don't think the feeling of humiliation has ever left me, I struggle with any confrontation, no I don't want a good argument! But I bottle things up and become very nervous and tearful if voices are raised even though I know that the person speaking is not violent.

Women who have escaped domestic violence often pay the price both emotionally and financially, moving often jeopardises continuity in employment. Health issues caused or exacerbated by the violence can often cause lifelong problems and tend to become worse as you get older. Years or even months of having you self-esteem battered makes making even simple decisions difficult if not impossible. New relationships need a really nice understanding man who is tolerant and patient. You will get insight into my little idiosyncrasies! You know who you are!

The jury is out regarding sex education but whilst the government are making progress in educating children on drug awareness no priory has been given to education on domestic violence, we need to educate our children. Maybe if children were aware of the facts, they would recognise the early signs, and be empowered to do something about it rather than feel the fear and humiliation that most victims do.

Men choose to be violent it's not caused by their team losing – it's something that they choose to do. Let's stop offering excuses/reasons for it such as a team losing or a difficult upbringing. We should be educating our children- both girls and boys. Police and domestic violence charities state that there is a rise in domestic violence during the football season. Whilst the police are to be commended for providing support for the expected increase in violence, we must not appear to imply that an increase in violence is part and parcel of the whole event. I believe that they should be clear about the consequences of any perpetrator of violence.

If you suspect someone is being abused please offer a helping hand or just a few kind words, I remember a young man approaching me when I was sitting on that bench having fled after the assault following the surgery on my nose, he approached the bench that I was sitting on and said "is there anything that I can do?, I don't know what's the matter but you look like a nice lady to me, can I phone anyone for you or get you anything?" I wish I had asked his name so that I could thank him, his kind words and caring approach really meant a lot when I was at rock bottom.

Message from Eve – Thank you so much for sharing your story with us, your pain came through and I cried but then such powerful and moving words as you plea with others at the end. Thank you. Take care and stay safe. Much respect to you. Eve x

CHAPTER TWENTY TWO

I was born in Mexico, my Mother had followed my Father back to his homeland and they married. My half brother was 6 at the time and suddenly found himself in a foreign land and enrolled in school. Our Mother had divorced his Father after 15 years due to her finding religion and reforming her alcoholic ways while her husband continued on with drinking and debauchery. My Father was not a drinker but as I understand it he was very controlling. Five years after marriage I came along, a year and a half after my birth my Grandma was in the final stage of terminal cancer. At this point my Mother decided to make a break and go back to Kansas to be with her dying Mother. My Father according to both my Mom and brother, would never let her have both of us at the same time, it was one or the other. So she left with my brother to the bus station with no intention of bringing me. Luckily my brother ran back to the hovel we lived in and sneaked me out the window, we made it to Kansas where things got complicated. My Father followed a few weeks later, staying in my Grandparents home long enough for them to call the INS and have him seized and deported, then my Grandma died, followed by my brothers Dad pulling shady strings to have him taken away by child services and given to him. My Mom was devastated; a legal battle raged for 3 years and ended when it went before the Kansas Supreme court. The ruling is still used to this day in judgment of child custody hearings involving religious choice differing among parents. The things that hurt me the most was the story of my brother having to rescue me in Mexico (She was going to leave me!) And I would hear her saying "I'm fit enough to take care of her but not her brother?" The child services left me in the home partly because the issue at hand involved my brothers Father and because legally I was a Mexican national.

Now to a young child there was a great feeling of not being wanted/loved, only now do I understand the situation for what it was. Once the case had settled and my brother was again with us my Mom found work and that was all she did, work, work and work. Seven days a week. Again my child mind thought that this work thing was more pleasant than being with me, so I basically raised myself in the comforts my Mother provided. I had become rather wild by 11, drinking, smoking and thieving from stores. She tried counseling, locking me up, locking me out and finally having me emancipated. Again, even after raising all the hell that I did, I assumed she just wanted rid of me. At 13 I was pregnant, the babies Daddy was 15 and a delinquent, he eventually got locked up when I was about 3 months along. When I was 7 months pregnant I met a construction worker 8 years my senior, he was charming, good looking and seemed to truly care about me. We moved in together and playing house was rather "Fun" neither one of us was very responsible or mentally mature. I had my son 3 months after turning 14, my Mother feared for the baby and threatened me with child services, so I gave in and let her keep him.

I had been with Jack about 6 months when the violence, insults and manipulation began. By this time we had moved to another state and I was alone, He began drinking more and more, working less and hurting me daily with slaps, shoves and verbal taunts. He knew my past and my fear of rejection; it was all used against me. When I became pregnant I thought it would make things better, how wrong I was. He accused me of cheating, of lying, of trying to trap him. During the pregnancy there was only verbal abuse, the physical aspect had stopped and gave me hope. When I had our Son we were staying with his co-workers and drinking buddies, basically homeless. He would disappear, I found out he was screwing the neighbor downstairs and I decided to call my Mom and she came to get me. I had over the next couple of weeks Jack called and called, promising the moon and stars. He wanted me back; he knew he had done wrong, that he would change. I bought it; my Mom would not let me take my oldest child; that hurt so bad. It was only a week after returning that the physical abuse started again, this time worse, this time punches were thrown. I felt so stupid and trapped! When the baby was 4 months old Jack chocked him out for spitting out baby food, then he performed CPR and got him breathing again. I was terrified, confused and felt helpless. I finally talked my Mom into letting me have my oldest come live with me, I lied and told her Jack had quit drinking and was doing good. I felt great, I loved and enjoyed motherhood, my boys were angels and reason to trudge on in life. I did my best to shelter them from the madness but the situation was awful. Again I became pregnant, I found myself 17 and with 3 young children. My daughter was healthy and beautiful; I had worried because Jack had physically abused me all through my pregnancy with her. By this time we were staying with my Mother, She had kicked him out numerous times but the law in the small town was a joke. Eventually we moved back out of state. Things got to the point where Jack would spend his check on drinking, drugs and women. I got to the point that I was glad he would leave, we were at peace and happy with him gone. In the end, after 10 years of this emotional roller coaster I caught him with a hooker on our sons Birthday and something snapped; I was done. By this time the kids as well as myself were damaged emotionally, I was not able to deal with the wreckage of the past, the confusion of the present or to see hope in the future. I began a decent into drugs that lasted 8 years of my life; I am both embarrassed and appalled at my actions and choices during that time. I had entered into another relationship where I was the abuser; I was the one hissing terrible words. Of course down the road the tables turned and my partner proved to be better at the sickness of abuse.

Ten years again. The turning point of my life and awakening of my inner strength came when I was sentenced to drug court, my first week in the program I found out I was pregnant, my youngest was 15 at the time. I found strength I thought I had lost, I was reading again, doing things I enjoy and Through the Twelve Steps I found peace. During this time the babies Daddy was still using, coming and going as he pleased.

It was not until he cussed me and disrespected me the day my Mother died that I found the will to cut him loose. Up until that point I had been holding the belief that people can change, I did. I am now without a partner; I have grown even more through reflection, faith and meditation. I do not see myself with anyone in the near or far future, I am not bitter or cold, I just know that after 20 years of being with 2 men that hurt me, disrespected me and manipulated me I need some serious time just getting to know and love me. I feel the best I have ever felt. I am over the sentence of misery that I gave myself all those years ago; I am over letting anyone/anything dominate my mind, body and life.

Message from Eve – What a brave, brave lady you are! You have survived! You have succeeded! Much respect to you, I admire your honesty so much and I pray that you continue on the path you have chosen. Stay strong. Eve x

CHAPTER TWENTY THREE

It began only three years ago and ended 6 months ago. I don't feel that I've wasted two and a half years; I don't feel let down by my past. After talking to Eve I now use it to gain strength and I know that there are hurdles out there but I can succeed, I can be a survivor. Here's my story.

He was the new recruit and after seeing him for the first time I knew I didn't stand a chance, he was gorgeous, what would he see in plain old me when Gerry was busy flashing her fake eyelashes at him.

Rob was put on my till so that I could show him the ropes and I couldn't help but get embarrassed whenever I spoke to him. By the end of our shift he had asked me to the pub after work and within a few weeks we were an item.

Rob told me that his parents were really rich and that he had to get a job to prove that he could work at a low level before he could be employed into the family banking business. I was impressed and when he took me home to meet his parents I was really in awe, their house was massive and really posh. Within two months I had given in my notice at the supermarket and moved in with Rob, he had two homes, a really neat apartment and a wing at his parent's house. We would lie in bed and smoke pot and laugh at how funny it was him working at the supermarket when his family had all that money. I'd never tried pot or any other drug for that matter before I met Rob but I liked the way it made me feel, all relaxed so I could share my secrets and dreams as we quickly fell in love.

By the six month period we were engaged and continued to live together. I was really happy but also really bored, I hated staying at home all day even though the luxury surroundings, new clothes, endless amounts of jewellery and pretty things did help a little but I was going crazy being in the house all day and so I asked Rob who by this time had left the supermarket and started work within his father's firm if I could get a job or perhaps go back to school. The punch to my face knocked me to the ground and the next thing I knew I was lay on the bed naked with Rob on top of me raping me.

I tried to scream but he clamped his hand over my mouth before grabbing at me with his other hand, it was quick, he rolled off me and walked off to the bathroom whilst I huddled in a ball sobbing my heart out.

I hated him, I wanted to kill him but I knew I didn't stand a chance. Over the months as I gradually got introduced to the families friends I quickly worked out that Rob and his parents had friends in high places and that money talked, who the hell would believe me.

Rob came back to bed as if nothing happened, kissed me on the cheek, turned over and went to sleep – this was the pattern of the rest of my relationship until he beat me so badly that his mother had to take me to the hospital. I knew I had to lie and so I gave the hospital staff the story that had been fed to me word by word and lay recovering from my injuries after surgery to my stomach to stop the internal bleeding.

Rob came to see me always playing the vigilant and caring fiancé, I hated him but I hated his mother more! That evil cow was covering for her son, my face was a mess, my nose broken, my eyes bruised and cut, my teeth knocked out, my cheekbone broken and all she did was stand at the bottom of my hospital bed and smile for the benefit of the nurses and doctors promising that she would do everything within her power to catch the culprit who had beaten her son's fiancé so badly.

As I recovered I knew what I had to do, I rang an old friend and asked him and his girlfriend to come and rescue me, I left the hospital without telling anyone and went into hiding.

I never went back; I relocated to the other side of the country, far away from Rob, his parents and his money. I realize now that he was very clever, he bought me, seduced me with his charm and wealth and I fell for it, I was naïve and gullible, stupid and young.

I've taken all that and turned it into something positive after speaking with Eve and I want to say a big thank you to her for allowing me this opportunity to share my story. It has helped me so much sharing this part of my life and I am now ready to continue my life as a survivor.

I must admit that the Fifty Shades Of Grey books were a very personal trigger for me. Christian Grey is an abuser; he seduced Ana with his wealth and charm just like Rob did with me. Okay the similarities end there and I don't mind the sex you write about but please EL James see your character for what he is, see your books for what they are abuse not romance.

Message from Eve – Brave lady. I am so happy you are free and a survivor and I am so glad that I have been able to not only help you but provide you with this opportunity to heal. May your progress continue. Respect. Eve x

CHAPTER TWENTY FOUR

My name is Beth and I am in my early 20s. I have decided to write my story to help others who experience domestic violence. I was a victim of domestic violence at the young age of 17 and suffered at the hands of my partner for two years until I fell pregnant with my first child. When I realized that I was pregnant, I gathered the strength and the courage to seek help.

The first time that my boyfriend hit me, I hit him back. Following the argument, we both said sorry and that we would never do it again so I thought nothing of it and told no one. As time went on it did happen again and it got gradually worse. Although I knew it was wrong I didn't want to believe that someone who loved me could hurt me that much and so I started to think that I deserved it. I lost all confidence and became really weak and so I didn't have the strength to tell anyone what was going on.

The longer I left it hoping it would get better it got worse and harder and harder to leave. When I fell pregnant I was so determined to protect myself and the baby that I left him. I was still very weak and would meet up with him when he suggested it. I was carrying his baby and I was scared of being alone. When I was five months pregnant he got angry one day and threw a bike at me. This was the last straw and I left. I saw him again a few months later when I was feeling stronger.

I felt that I could keep it together and have an adult conversation about the baby. When he arrived I could tell that he still had issues with anger and when he started throwing things I saw the signs that he was going to get violent with me. I made the decision to hit him before he hit me in hindsight I wish I hadn't done this but I was so determined that he wasn't going to hit me again and hurt my unborn child. He was so shocked at my new found strength that he called the police and had me arrested! Since then he has spent time in prison for the abuse he inflicted on me. It was a long and difficult process trying to regain my confidence and find myself again as domestic violence is something that takes a long time to get over. This is why I decided to put a book together to try and help other people out there, who are also experiencing DV,

If you are in an abusive relationship you are not alone. I want to try to persuade young women to get help. If you think you know someone who may be experiencing DV pass my booklet to them and encourage them to seek help. As someone who experienced DV at such a young age I know how it feels to be victim and how lonely it can feel, It is now three years since I gout out of my abusive relationship and I am a much stronger person. I don't want to let horrible experience affect my happiness in life; instead, I want to use it to help others. Even if I can't help everyone who reads my book I hope it can persuade you that you are not alone and encourage you to find the power to seek help.

Beth x

Message from Eve – Yet another courageous young lady who wants to use her experiences to help others. Thank you for sharing your story. Eve x

CHAPTER TWENTY FIVE

I was 31 when I met Tony, he was gorgeous thick blonde wavy hair and blue eyes just my type.

We got cozy very quickly and I'm embarrassed to say that he managed to get me into bed on the first night. The sex was drunken and wild and when I woke up the next morning I remember hiding my face. I'd never had a one night stand before and because we hadn't really talked I didn't know where I stood with him. It wasn't long before I knew exactly where I stood with Tony!

Within a week he'd moved himself and his belongings into my apartment, I was happy most of my friends had met him, I had a very small but close circle of mates some of who I'd known since pre school and they all liked him and thought we looked really good together.

Tony worked long hours he was a solicitor and he would often come home stressed, he'd given his rented apartment up when he moved in with me and even though I was falling in love with him his moods started to really irritate me especially when I had had a stressful day at work, I was a social worker. Every day I visited homes, a huge percentage of my cases were domestic violence and so the last thing I needed after a really troublesome day was Tony moaning about a case he'd lost.

One night his mood was particularly bad and so grabbing my gym stuff I made for the door shouting over my shoulder that I would be back soon. I didn't make it out of the door.

I felt the yanking of my hair as he pulled me forcefully backwards toppling me over I hit my head on the floor. When I woke up I had never felt pain like it, my whole face throbbed but burnt the pain was so intense and my skin felt warm and wet. I remember reaching up to my face and feeling my cheek my cries becoming hysterical as I saw the blood on my fingers, there was so much.

Somehow I managed to stand up my whole body was painful where he had kicked and stamped on me and the blood was gushing from my nose and eyebrow, Tony had smashed my face to a pulp, I was unrecognizable.

I don't remember going to the hospital, my friend rang the ambulance after she found me on the floor, Tony rang her crying saying I had fallen down the stairs. For the first few days whilst I was in hospital he tried to text and ring me so I turned my phone off but not before ringing the police. I gave a statement the embarrassment there for everyone to see, you see for months Tony had been abusing me, punching me, kicking me but because of my job I was too ashamed to admit that I was one of the women I worked with every day and so I hid the bruises as best as I could and the ones I couldn't I explained to friends and colleagues that I had fallen or bumped myself! I should have known better, I should have walked away but I didn't! This time though I knew better Tony had gone too far. My nose was broken, I had no teeth in the front of my mouth, my face was a mess but what hurt the most was the scar that ran down the side of my face where he sliced me with a knife and never ever will I see out of my left eye again.

I'm now a nervous wreck, I gave my job up because I just couldn't cope with the stress, I now sympathize too much with the women I have to visit and it kills me! I don't like to leave my flat, I gave my apartment up, I couldn't settle there and I didn't feel safe so now I live in a secure little flat and I've had CCTV installed and every security measure I can think of. I take a cocktail of pills every day just to exist and another lot before I get into bed at night. I sleep on average 3-6 hours a day, mainly when it's light and always better if a friend comes and stays over. I'm a mess but I'm alive. I like Eve was lucky, I walked away but I know there are many who don't. I'm no longer embarrassed I want to help and so I share my story with you all.

Thank you Eve for giving me this opportunity and I hope that your dream becomes a reality. You are an amazing woman who has really inspired me and helped me so much.

I am a survivor!

Message from Eve – Thank you so much, your kind words really inspire me to try to do more and I am so happy that I have been able to help you. Stay safe and keep smiling. Always here. Eve x

CHAPTER TWENTY SIX

Thank you for this opportunity, here is my story.

I was 16 when I met my husband and having been brought up in a very strict house I was very innocent. My parents did things the old fashioned way, dad went out to work and mum stayed home and looked after the house and family. She taught us girls well, by the age of 11 I could iron a man's shirt and trousers and making a bed was a piece of cake. Mum always used to say "the way to a man's heart is through his stomach" and "if you look after your man he will look after you." I took her words as gospel and watched from the sidelines always with a smile whenever my dad took my mum around the waist, whispering in her ear she would giggle before they kissed briefly always aware that there were six kids running around the house the kiss was always quick but I always knew that my parents loved one another deeply. As I grew older I wanted the same, I wanted what my mum had and so I vowed that I would be the best wife a man could ever want when I was old enough to get married, I would be just like my mum!

Phil was charming and he respected my innocence. Within 6 months we were engaged with the wedding set for the next summer, I was excited I would be barely 17 when we wed.

My mum and dad paid the deposit on a house for us and in the July we got married and after a short honeymoon in Brighton we returned to our new home.

I looked after my man and my home just the way my mum had taught me to and every night I made sure there was a meal waiting for Phil when he came home from work. Within five months I was pregnant and it wasn't easy, I was very sick and this is when the violence and abuse started.

All day I had struggled to keep even the smallest amount of water down and so cooking my husband's dinner was the last thing on my mind. I was curled up on the sofa when he arrived home from work and as soon as he saw me I knew I was in trouble.

He didn't beat me badly, I think he was afraid because I was pregnant but I learnt my lesson, never again would I be a bad wife and let him down.

As my tummy grew I struggled to fit into my clothes. I didn't have any money of my own and so I asked Phil. I'm sorry I did. He didn't hit me at first; he grabbed my arm and took me upstairs to our bedroom where he flung open the wardrobe ripping all my clothes off the hangers before throwing them all over the bed and floor. He was cussing and shouting and every so often he grabbed me by the hair when he wanted to home in a point.

I didn't ask for money again but I did borrow my mum's sewing machine to alter some of my clothes and repair the damage to those Phil had ripped when he tore them from their hangers.

I became quite the seamstress over the next few months and as my belly grew I would alter the clothes all over again.

Phil seemed happier and as my due date approached I sighed with relief every night when my head hit the pillow, I was exhausted and marveled at how my mum had coped with all of us, I hadn't even had one yet and I was shattered! Phil didn't want sex much these days, he said my body was disgusting and so I tried to hide it away beneath long nightdresses, I don't think Phil saw me naked from being about 3 months pregnant.

Patricia was born and from the minute I held her I was in love, she was so perfect and we named her after Phil's mum which is what he wanted so everyone was happy especially my mum when he said that Patricia could have her name as her middle name, Patricia May.

By the time Patricia was 6 months old I was pregnant again and just thankful that she was such a good baby. Phil again didn't come near me whilst I was pregnant and secretly I was happy I was so tired.

At 8 months pregnant I was diagnosed with breast cancer but denied treatment until my son was born, Nicholas was as cute as his sister with dark wavy hair and the biggest eyes I had ever seen but I was very ill and so Phil's mum had to jump in and help.

I had my treatment and Phil was ok through it, he laughed at me when my hair began to fall out but he didn't hit me as much and he hardly was home so I started to relax a bit and enjoy the peace trying to make myself better for my kids.

Two days before Christmas and whilst I was pregnant with our third child a woman knocked on my front door, she worked with Phil and told me that for the last three years they had been having an affair. Through every pregnancy, my fight with cancer, everything, I was destroyed. All the beatings, all the cruel words and I had tried my best to be perfect for him yet he'd done this to me, to us.

Phil walked through the front door just as I was calming myself down, I'd cried for over two hours, he knew. He didn't talk to me just walked up the stairs, packed a suitcase and left. I've never seen him since and I don't want to. He doesn't bother with the kids, oh he sends money every so often which I am really grateful for but he doesn't want any contact, he's started a fresh life. When Lucy Rose was born he didn't come to the birth and he's never seen her. I've sent photographs to his mum's and asked her to pass them on because none of this is my children's fault and he is still their father. I hope one day he misses them too much and wants to see them but until then I am mum and dad to our three children.

As for me I will never trust anyone again, I've sat for hours picking apart my marriage blaming myself but now I no longer do. I'm working hard to make a good life for my children and myself and it's bloody hard, I struggle for money and have to claim disability, the cancer and beatings have left me very poorly and I'm worried about the future. Here in England we have a new government, I don't know much about politics but I do know he is wrecking our country and leaving people like me to suffer. I struggle enough as it is to heat the house and put food on the table and now he wants to take that away from us, I honestly don't know what the future holds for me and my children but I love them with all my heart and put every ounce of energy into them.

Please don't suffer tell someone, I wish I had.

Message from Eve – Brave, brave lady. I wish you and your children happiness every day for the rest of your lives. May you grow stronger and continue on your survivor's journey. I'm here. Eve x

CHAPTER TWENTY SEVEN

I was pregnant with my second child when my partner first hit me. My daughter who was two at the time was holding my hand when he punched me to the floor but luckily she wasn't hurt.

My daughter is from another relationship, a disastrous one which ended with my running away after he had beaten me for most of the 11 months. I didn't know I was pregnant when I left but my daughter is the best thing ever to happen to me and even though me and her dad are now friends and he has gone on to help me so much I still don't trust him.

I find this hard to admit but I blamed myself, I had had two relationships and both men had hit me, what was I doing wrong? Naomi's dad said I was "gobby" I thought I was standing up for myself and my new partner, the father of my second baby said it too and so I tried really hard to keep my mouth shut.

For the remainder of my relationship with Justin's dad, Justin is my son, my second child; he hit me, verbally abused me and belittled me. I felt useless, ugly and fat. I didn't bother to put on make up anymore, there was no point I never went anywhere except to the supermarket and my hair was a mess usually scrapped back into a ponytail. I hadn't bought any new clothes in ages, I didn't have the money but as long as my kids didn't go without I was happy.

I put up with every punch, every slap, every kick. I've had my tea poured over my head, a hot drink thrown at me, my fingers burnt on the stove, my hair cut, my eyebrows shaved off, he even tried to slice my nipple off with a Stanley knife blade. Every visit to the hospital or doctors he was there and I knew every time what I had to say, I was a clumsy fool.

The last time he attacked me was a Friday night, he been out with his mates and was leathered when he came home. He stunk but wanted sex and so I let him wanting him to just get it over with so he would go to sleep, he couldn't get an erection and so blamed me. He tore my hair from my head, handfuls at a time and I could feel my scalp bleeding, he punched and kicked me as he dragged me from the bed down the stairs into the living room. I was beaten to within an inch of my life but do you know who saved me? Naomi's father the first man who ever hit me! My clever daughter had crept out of bed and went into my room to get my mobile phone, she then sneaked back into her room and rang her daddy texting him until he arrived and kicked in the front door the police not far behind him. I don't remember any of it my head hit the fireplace as he threw me down and to this day I don't recall anything after that, I'm glad for that.

Naomi's dad saved me, he saved us and now he's my best friend. He was brave and sought help and he's almost finished with his therapy. He's a changed man but I will never forget what he too is capable of, I will never be able to trust him 100%.

Message from Eve – Another very courageous woman. The fear never truly goes away and as survivors we learn not to trust, a sad but very true fact. Much respect to you. Stay safe. Your friend. Eve

CHAPTER TWENTY EIGHT

My name is Wayne and I am Naomi's daddy and even though I am nervous about writing this story I hope it will help others. I saw that the way I was acting, the way I was treating people, especially women was wrong, I had no respect and so I went to see my doctor and I was honest, I told him the whole truth and he referred me for specialist help. I've been seeing my therapist for a while now and I can't remember the last time I lost my temper. Life is good; I'm learning every day and my daughter, Justin and Belinda are my world.

I hurt Belinda badly but I have always loved her and I know she will never trust me again but I will always be around for her.

When I was a kid I was a little shit to be honest, where there was trouble there was me. I had my first tattoo at 13 and got the hiding of my life when I went home proudly showing off my inked arm to my brothers. I was always fighting, showing everyone on the estate who was boss. I thought I was hard and when Belinda wouldn't do as her told it made me mad, she would go on and on winding me up until I snapped. At the time I can't tell you how much pleasure I used to get from feeling her hair wrapped round my fingers or her hand reach up to try to get me to let go now I feel disgust, disgusted that I was a monster that got a kick out of hurting the woman I said I loved, the mother of my baby.

Whenever she cried I would mimic her, her crying did my head in and just made me get even madder now I hate seeing her cry it hurts me, it hurts my heart.

I want her to be happy but I know she needs space. I take the kids out for her to the park and MacD's and Justin is a great kid who I treat no different than Naomi.

I know that for the rest of my life I will have to fight the monster that is inside me but I would rather kill myself than hurt another woman ever again! I've changed and I'm proud of the man I have become. Women should be respected at all times and believe me men if you don't love and treat your woman right you may just regret it because there are good men I'm now one of them.

Message from Eve – Thank you, thank you, thank you. When you first approached me by email and asked if you could submit a chapter for the book I must admit I was apprehensive but I strongly belief that every side of domestic violence/abuse needs to be in the spotlight and so I welcome the addition of your story with open arms. You have shown a great deal of bravery by seeking help and then sharing and may you continue on the right path, the path of peace and hope. Respect. Eve x

CHAPTER TWENTY NINE

My Lost Youth

If someone had of told me a few years ago that I'd be writing my story I would have laughed in their faces! But here I am writing it, never in my wildest dreams did I ever think that My story would be one of Domestic Violence and now Mental Health and one that will live with me forever!!!!

Ok so it was summer of 1992 I was fourteen not long turned actually and I remember being excited about being on holiday from school. I went to a school in south London I wasn't very good at school academically but I went all the same that was soon to be brought to a sudden end. I was a happy go lucky girl yeah family had problems drink, no money, mum and dad didn't really get on but still life was ok. One day I was out playing with friends I grew up with these 'friends' always together, causing mischief, annoying the neighbours we were young and living life. I was in my denim cut off dungarees and a belly top and not long been subjected to wearing braces!!! See I was a shy girl with no confidence no one have ever seen me in shorts I could feel my confidence building the more compliments I was gaining, everybody dressed like that then. We didn't have a care in the world even if we had, being outside with friends was our escape I suppose and we loved it.

A few weeks later me and a friend were sitting in the play park just talking, she was a few years older than me when a man walked passed she said HI to him, I remember asking who he was as I hadn't seen him before she explain that it was a friend and she known him through somebody else that we both knew. I didn't take much notice as I wasn't interested in boys etc and he was much older than me. A few hours later we were playing a silly game can't remember what it was but I remember chasing people and vice versa along he popped and through everyone else he ended up playing the game, while writing this I can see now how odd that must sound and to be honest you'd be right! So while playing this game that he was now playing he decided that by calling me a 'tart' that it would spur me on to chase him which it did. As I chased him he went in to a block, underneath there were sheds that were partitioned by brick wall. As I got further in I started to call him he didn't answer I knew he was there so I walked further in not really being able to see anything. I peered around the wall slightly nervous when suddenly he grabbed me pushed me against the wall and began kissing me... (I'd never kissed a boy until then). I was shocked to say the least. Why he had done that? I mean I'm 14 he's 21 why would he be interested in me?? I always thought he wanted my friend...he knew how old I was because just a little while before we were doing names and ages etc. I walked out of there shocked thinking OMG I've never kissed anyone before he's had many woman bet he thought I was shit! I ran out to tell my friend what had just happened she was as shocked as I was. He began coming around everyday after that grabbing me when he could to have a sneaky kiss I suppose I was flattered me being 14 and him an older man chasing me. I didn't class us as being boyfriend and girlfriend because he hadn't asked me (thought that's how it was meant to happen?) and I was so young. I hadn't seen him all day then he turned up out of the blue as he usually did and again I was sitting in the park with my friends and sister, he sat on top of the climbing frame it was like a spider web with lots of red thick rope, he called me over I climbed up trying to sit down when he pushed me I lost my footing falling in to the ropes scraping my arms and face...my friends hadn't seen him push me and obviously started laughing he gave me a look a look that said keep your mouth shut. I stuck to them same story 'id fell'. Alarm bells should have started ringing but didn't think anything of it......

A few weeks later I can remember him asking me too go back in and change my clothes as my friends were taking the piss out of me, I was devastated to think I was being laughed at of course they wasn't he didn't like me showing any skin. So I did I went in and changed and remember mum asking why I was dressed for winter when it was boiling hot outside! He would say it's because he loved me and wanted to protect me. Yep! I fell for that I wanted that. He told me he loved me very early on. He made me feel special. He was very eager to let everyone know that we were an item I was confused I had been told not to tell anyone but seen as he loved me I assumed he wanted the world to know, he began by telling his cousin who was so shocked she thought we were joking. He made it clear that it wasn't a joke. We were already friends so she just accepted it. Told mum and the family think mum already knew though...well mum was over the moon she thought he was a nice man, she knew the family and had done for years as did my dad....so he would come round everyday after school we'd watch TV he'd have dinner and then he went home everything was going well apart from school had a massive falling out over something really silly and ended up not wanting to go to school.....it became a nightmare. I went to school sometimes but felt like I was hated so id bunked off, looking back I don't think I was but I had changed he was having an effect on me. He quickly began to tell me where and when I went out, I had to look out of my bed room window until he came round wasn't allowed out until then and sometimes he wouldn't even show up. So the relationship carried on like that until I turned fifteen, the day I turned 15 my life changed forever.

It was my 15th birthday I was in a brilliant mood, previous to this a mutual friend of ours said he would get me a birthday card because he had forgotten the years before we made a joke of it saying he'll forget that year too and he did so he came round with a small box of chocolates, he felt bad for not getting the card gave him a cuddle to say thank you that's when HE snapped he asked if he could speak to me I kinda felt from him that he wasn't happy he had a certain look he gave when wasn't happy anyway he took me round the corner away from everyone else, no sooner did I get round the corner he grabbed me by the throat and began punching me in the face and being accused of 'FUCKING OUR FRIEND' how? I wasn't allowed out? I screamed out shouting at him when our friend came round and see that he had me pinned up against the wall a massive fight broke out between the two of them and of course it was my fault...oh I was the biggest bitch slut slag I was every horrible name you can think off...I kept my mouth shut.

Mum and dad had split up by this time so it was just us...mum had a day job but also began working at night cleaning so I would look after my brother and sister.

So mum left for work and she shouted up to the window said she was going and there was to be no arguing between me and him. I reassured mum that we would be fine. I came in shut the window holding on to the handle of the window I wished I had gone with mum, instinct is a great thing and my instincts told me something bad was about to happen!! I wracked my brains wondering what I could have done to make him angry I couldn't think of anything. I was well trained by then I knew what and not to say, I had even mastered the tone in which I spoke to him as that would often piss him off. It didn't matter any way he needed no excuse as I was about to find out. so I came in letting go off the handle he was sat on my single bed and had an awful look in his eye grinding his teeth here we go he was angry. I got to the point where id rather he just hit me and get it over and done with rather than wait for a slap or a punch and the abuse to go with it. Any way he told me to sit down on the bed which I did he smiled I smiled back hoping it would settle him, he got up and went downstairs closing my bedroom door behind him 'phew' id thought it was ok. My sister and her friend were in the front room talking I thought he'd gone to speak to them as he often did ha-ha silly me!! I could hear the front room curtains being shut, the kitchen window being slammed shut and locked…and my sister asking what the hell he was doing, he didn't answer her and I daren't move as he had told me to stay sat on the bed. I heard the street door being locked up the chain, the bolts going across. He came in to my bedroom hand behind his back. He came over to me and began kissing me my brains doing over time. He told me to lie down on the bed when he brought a big meat knife out and held it against my throat pushing it harder and harder in to my skin. I began crying when he said 'take them off' meaning my trousers!!! I begged him not to do it pleading with him he gave me an ice cold stare I began to undo my trousers...all the time the knife is being pushed in further and further. I prayed so hard for someone to help me, he suddenly jumped up running downstairs shouting 'Quick call an ambulance I've killed her' my sister came running up to see me lying on the bed trousers down sobbing quietly, I had perfected that too. About half an hour later his cousin came down and asked if we wanted to go to the cinema I said I didn't want to as I wasn't feeling well, he made me go during the film he kept asking if I loved him? Why didn't I love him? I kept saying I did and everything was fine. walking back from the cinema his cousin her boyfriend were going to the kebab shop she asked me if I wanted anything/ before I could answer he shouted 'NO she's not eating she can watch us' and that I did and it stayed that way until I left him.

Not long after that I realized I hadn't came on yep you guessed it I was pregnant and devastated looking back on it, there was never any talk of contraception hmmmmmm wonder why? Anyway there's me pregnant in my school uniform devastated he made it clear I was to get rid as he put it. I plucked up the courage to tell my aunt who then told my mum. I walk in in my school uniform mum must have been devastated (as a parent I can see that now). eventually I had know choice but to go ahead with the abortion I remember it like it was yesterday completely devastated doing something I didn't want to do. Everybody said it was for the best and he made sure that it went ahead. The whole thing from start to finish was a nightmare I could barely walk after I had to be held up by my mum and aunt I got home and slept for a few hours. (Obviously because I had fallen pregnant mum was fuming with him, so he wasn't allowed round to the house any more he didn't seem to care I suppose he got what he wanted). I had to go and see him just wanted him to hold me and tell me it was going to be ok, I spent an hour looking for him, eventually I found him in the bookies I caught his attention he came out and asked me what I wanted? BASTARD!!! Never felt so lost. No cuddle, no are you ok? Just cold...I could almost see the disgust in his face. I walked away feeling alone helpless and that the whole world was against me. I can remember begging my mum not to tell my dad as I knew if he knew war would begin, I later learnt that dad had warned Him not to touch me in any way, he couldn't help himself! It was almost as if he had set out to do the things he was doing, he controlled me in every single way....clothes, thoughts, feelings, friendships, relationships. He eventually turned me against my family had no relationship with them what so ever well apart from the arguments and believe me there were loads, by this time dad was coming back at weekends everything around me was going wrong. No school, No friends or family he had taken everything away he was a very clever man. he would plant the seed almost by saying see no one loves you like I do they've all gone and I'm still here, I clung to him even more, scared of being completely alone.

Things went from being a secret to him showing his true side this was the first time my sister had seen him hit me...my mum had gone to work and me and my sister were at home mum left us some money to get some chips for lunch, my sister went to the cafe around the corner she must have been back 5 minutes when there was a knock at the door he knew mum was at work…his face when he see me eating. He asked where his was before I could answer BANG a massive slap to the face, I quickly realised it was because he hadn't given me permission to eat!!!! That's when my eating quickly became a problem; my weight became so low my doctor was considering putting me in to hospital to build me back up. I didn't go into hospital I promised id start eating properly and get back to being healthy me again HA who was I kidding? He came back a few hours later saying how sorry he was and he loved me blah blah blah. He said I was to meet him at a certain time as he wanted me to go some where with him but wouldn't say where I did as I was told. I lived in a very rough area where drug dealers would just stand around asking if you wanted anything. So I met him and he said he had to meet someone at a pub I knew of the pub because it was well known for that sort of thing… drugs. so I was stood out side a shoe shop waiting for him it was cold and dark and I was shitting myself I was there for a while wondering if he had just left me there it wouldn't surprise me see I was used to all this now! I remember thinking 5 more minutes and I'm going, well as I turned around he was running towards me with what must have been 5 men shouting and running after him he handed me this ball of stuff told me to run…..the men were getting closer I ran for my life he was no where to be seen I managed to hide from them I could hear them shouting and swearing. I stayed where I was too scared to move when I heard him calling me. He took me to a lift shaft I gave him the ball of stuff I knew not to question him, I just watched. He had a plastic bottle, foil and a lighter he began to burn this stuff id never seen anything like it before…….yep he was on drugs! Crack cocaine to be exact, and the men that were after me were the drug dealers he had just scammed. I began to shake and feel sick he couldn't have given a shit that they could have caught me could have done anything to me. I began to feel angry for the first time I see him for what he was a no good drug taking arsehole who was taking advantage of a 14 year old. From then on he was constantly high asking me to find the money for him!!! Id pretends that I had asked but no one had it. You see he didn't work and relied on his DSS money and of course that all went on drugs. He didn't have his own flat either and was going from couch to couch he asked me to spend the night with him one night yeah I answered thinking it would never happen as we had know where to go? Ha-ha how silly was I thinking we had no where to go, yep it was freezing cold snowing in fact when he took me to show me where we going to stay. I knew this place it wasn't a house or a bedroom oh no that would have been to nice for me. It was in fact it was a boiler room, according to him it was safe and warm and some where we could be together...he failed to notice the dirt rubbish and the spiders. I didn't want another beating these were becoming so frequent now, a day didn't go past where he hadn't slapped me or punched me and the calling of names well I answered to slag. I remember that in between all this my dad and his family were always at each other because of me being pregnant my nerves were in bits. NIGHTMARE! my mum was trying to send me away to my uncles he lived out of London secretly I wanted to go, I needed the break I didn't want to be in this anymore. so I told him what the plan was and of course he hated it he knew I wouldn't come back after hours of arguing he made me go and phone my uncle I knew he'd be listening so I pretended to be having a conversation with him when I went back out he said two words 'good girl' secretly inside I was laughing and it felt good.

He soon found out that I was going to go to my uncles how he found these things out I'll never know, he said that I had made him look stupid and I'll pay for it and that I did. I was sitting outside on a wall on the estate everyone was there he came up too me smiling he grabbed hold of my shirt and ripped it open I was stood there with everything on show I can hear the laughter now. I done my shirt back up and continued to sit on the wall he was calling me all sorts of names and though anger I shouted your mums a prostitute I jumped of the wall getting ready to run when he came running up and fly kicked me in the back causing my face to smash against the corner of the wall I was sitting on......I blacked out. I awoke to people calling me and a girl cuddling me I don't know who she was, I got up in a daze when my friend started screaming that my eye was hanging out (she had slightly exaggerated)....she quickly rushed me to her Nan's house who put frozen peas on it I couldn't see for a while and that side of my face was black he also managed to fracture my nose I still have the marks. Things quickly became out of control then.

I didn't go to my uncles after all...he had won again.....my feelings were beginning to change towards him. The embarrassing thing was that everyone knew what he was doing to me but not once did I hear leave him. Most people were scared of him. We didn't have mobiles so he would mainly contact me through others sending them to the door....mum would forbid me to go but his word was much stronger than mums I had to go. Me and mum eventually stopped talking as I was loosing the plot...I was fighting and arguing with everyone. No one could reach out to me by now. I was a little girl angry lost and scared. this went on for a few more months made me run away threatening to take me away to where he grew up..winding me to the point of passing out it was so bad once that he had beat me up thrown bricks at me when I fell he kicked me in the back he thought he had killed me...wish he had at this point. Mum reported him to the police but couldn't do anything as I wouldn't give a statement.

My uncle had moved not far from where we were staying he didn't know what was going on until he came round he was an alcoholic so was aware of much, H e had sent someone to come and knock for me, I was cooking dinner as mum was at work, I couldn't go out and being honest I didn't want too..He got so angry he began throwing bricks at the street door. I had truly had enough by now. any way so I began feeling unwell again and yes I was once again pregnant this time was different I was going to stick my guns and have this baby whether they like it or not. Of they didn't but I couldn't careless. I told him that I was pregnant again and keeping it he was angry that I had made a decision, I also plucked up the courage to tell him that unless he stopped hitting me we couldn't be together, as you can imagine he was livid but I didn't care. I was on my way to see my Nan with a friend and my sister when he popped up again asking me to speak to him. I told him I couldn't I was on my way out. We got in to an argument nothing new there. he kept going on about me being pregnant and it being his baby I snapped and told him to fuckoff (how brave was I?) when he raised his foot trying to kick me in my stomach I'll never forget his words 'IF YOU DONT WANT ME YOU ARE NOT HAVING MY BABY' I was more determined than ever.

My uncle who I mentioned earlier put me in touch with a solicitor and I got an injunction out on him, he was served the injunction came around to my house and ripped it up in front of me...I knew then it was final. Except it wasn't really...I lived in fear of him seeing me with the baby and taking him. I kept my child away from that monster he will never see him!

So now I live with my 2 beautiful children life should be good, but because of him I now live with depression and PTSD life has been very tough and still is because of the mental health. I fight every day as a result of him.

BUT I SMILE BECAUSE I AM FREE.

Message from Eve – PTSD is sadly very common in victims of domestic violence/abuse and so when this brave lady asked if MIND could be her nominated charity I happily agreed even though it isn't strictly a domestic violence charity.

You have fought very hard and I am so happy that even though sharing your story caused you initial pain you have come through this a stronger more empowered woman! RESPECT! Your friend. Eve x

CHAPTER THIRTY

I am a male immigrant from the Middle-East to Canada and a survivor of domestic violence. This is my story.

I dated my ex-wife for a few years as I was going through immigration process we waited until I was accepted and then married; our first days as a married couple were also our first days in Canada.

It was not even a month that she started to attack me. We could not find jobs and she was very angry. She punched me on the face and I tried to contain her. I had never seen such a thing before, I was very unfamiliar with domestic violence but her attacks worried me a lot. I called a 'couple counselling' therapist and we started to go. The therapist, after hearing our situation said to me "This is going to be very difficult for you; you may want to leave her." He also said that I was "passive-aggressive" in the way that I handled the problem.

I decided that I would do my best to help her. She was under pressure of immigration and poverty, so she needed help. She, on the other hand, had apparently only heard the therapist's opinion about me being passive-aggressive so she started to say that since I was psychologically troubled I must just agree that she control everything and try to fix myself instead of complaining about her anger and violence.

Soon she refused to continue the therapy and her violence became more frequent. Every 4-5 days she started attacking me for no reason at all, punching me and kicking me, usually for what I had done a few days before, or for no reason. Once she simply punched me because as she said "Oh you men are so disgusting" after she had seen a report about paedophilia on TV. Her attacks made me very angry, and I usually hit her back. Then she came back to me for a make-up sex.

After a year I hated myself, our relationship was devastating me. Every few days she started the violence; she started by insults and ridicule, then moved on to punching me in the face and kicking me on legs or stomach, until I got very angry. I would hit her back or push her then she approached me for making peace and having sex. I was unable to resist her making me angry, and I was unable to resist her initiating sex. I hated being emotionally played like that and I hated myself for beating her when I was angry.

One night after a violent incident I could not stand it any more, I told her to call the police; I figured if they arrested both of us perhaps she would realize how bad the situation was. The police arrested both of us charging us with assault against each other. The court made us go through anger-management sessions. I was happy and hopeful because my plan seemed to be working, the arrest and anger-management was not something that I could not endure; it was definitely worth having a good marriage.

I do not know what program she went through, but it worked. She stopped her assaults on me. She continued her insult and ridicule and making me angry, and then having make-up sex, but without physical violence. Many times I decided to leave her, every time I thought to myself that she has an issue and I have to help her overcome it. When we didn't fight, everything was great.

Then we had a baby. I was very happy and I thought things would become better.

Unfortunately, I was very wrong. A few months after our daughter was born the violence came back; it became more dangerous because she threw different objects including knives at me. She also threatened the baby with violence. This time I was very worried, the anger management classes had told me that even if she attacks me, I should not hit her back, and I did not hit her back anymore. It was only she who attacked me regularly. And I just left the house or went to a room when she attacked me. After a while she suddenly came to me when I was in bed and hit me on the head with an empty bottle of rum, it became unbearable. I called the police and they arrested her. And such a big mistake it was.

They sent her to a center for domestic violence. In that center, they told her that the reason that women are violent to their husbands is because of abusive husbands, a woman would not be abusive otherwise. This was such an unfounded claim but she used it. After that she started accusing me of abuse. She said when I stop talking to her and go to my room it is a form of "emotional abuse", I said "perhaps if you didn't call me an idiot I wouldn't leave the conversation."

She also accused me of abuse because I had called the police. At this period in our marriage, I had made my decision to divorce her but I was worried for my child. She often threatened the 2 year old child with violence and she traumatized her by yelling and I could not leave the child with her, I consulted with different people and they said the child would not come to me after divorce and if I said about her behavior with the child to the authorities they would take away the child, but not give her to me. I stopped my relationship with her and moved to the basement apartment in our house to be close to the child. I also suffered from depression at this time and had suicidal tendencies.

Sometimes that the child needed me I would go upstairs, and her violence continued. She would beat me and I would go back to the apartment. One night the child had a fever and she yelled at the child scaring her. I went there and picked up the child and took her to another room and calmed her and put her to sleep. Then went to my ex-wife and confronted her. She pushed my face and hold my head to the wall yelling at me while her hand was pressing on my face with my head to the wall. When she was done with her speech and let my head go. I spat on her face, in return she spat on my face repeatedly.

She attacked me and scratched my neck very deeply with her finger nails. Then I went to the living room to call the police, she grabbed the phone and called the police, the police came, and arrested me for assault because of spitting. They did not even ask why I was bleeding, even though they recorded my wounds when I was in prison.

After this, the court sent me to a special program about domestic violence specific to the Middle-Eastern men. They claimed it was because of language but most men in that program could speak fluent English, a couple of them spoke English as first language because there were raised in Canada. In that program, even though I told them I was the victim and she scratched my neck and I only spat, they said it is you who has been arrested.

In this program, four people surrounded me and tried to convince me that everything was my fault because of my cultural background and male privilege. I was on anti-depressant pills and they knew about it very well. In my opinion it should be a crime to tell a depressed person with suicidal tendencies that all his problems are his own fault.

I believed them. They practically pushed me over the edge of insanity and they did it knowing that I was mentally unstable. I believed that I was a horrible and worthless person; I was depressed, weak, poor, unpleasant. She was the victim because she was a woman, I had a history of hitting her in the past and I was from a misogynist cultural back ground, that means that I was a wife-beater at heart according to these experts. I only tried to find an excuse to get angry with her, and her insults and attacks were because she was frustrated.

I went back to my house. Moved to the basement because I was physically unable to sleep with her, I had panic attacks during sex which made my mental problem even worse because I thought I was impotent and I even hated myself more. By this time I viewed myself as a worthless person who was good for nothing, was raised badly and was even impotent too, I deserved to be living like a slave in my own house. I tried to be a good supporter anyway because my daughter was the only reason left in the world to live. For two years I gave my ex-wife my pay checks and she only gave me the tokens to ride the subway to work. She beat me repeatedly, usually in front of my child and sometimes her mother who came to visit helped her in her assaults on me. I was completely mentally unstable. I would go to the basement and cry trying to convince myself to not commit suicide because of my daughter. She also yelled at our daughter and so many nights my daughter and I slept in the basement in my bed crying with each other. I did not know what to do. Once I left the house but I missed my daughter and I was afraid for her to be traumatized so I went back. My ex also repeatedly threatened me with false domestic abuse claim and putting me in jail.

She controlled all my credit cards as well, that made me completely broke. One night I asked her why she is not paying my credit card payment because the bank keeps calling me. She started yelling at me. I was supposed to take the child with me to my basement apartment, so I picked up the child to go, telling her "Let's go downstairs your mom is mad." That made her very angry and she started to beat me with a shoe while I was holding the child and her mother also yelled at me. I went to my own apartment still holding the child and she and her mother followed us into the apartment, beating me with a shoe. At this moment I completely lost my patience, I grabbed the phone and called the police; even if they took the child away it still would be better than this.

The police came, she and her mother both lied that it was me who slapped her. I was arrested and imprisoned but that was how I was rescued. After getting out of jail, I left the house, rented an apartment, met my child only once a week. It took me a few years to recover from depression but I finally did it. I also started dating other women and my panic attack that I had during sex gradually went away, turned out I am actually quite healthy. I also recovered from financial troubles. It saddens me that my daughter speaks to her mom in an aggressive way, they yell at each other and their communication is very dysfunctional with threat and manipulation and crying and yelling. But I try to provide a peaceful environment for my child and I am happy that when she is with me she is such a great girl. I meet her everyday, even though it is very costly and time-consuming but I know that if I don't meet her everyday it is too much of mental pressure for her. To be able to maintain the arrangement of meeting her everyday I have accepted a large monthly payment to my ex-wife. If I wanted to settle in the court I would not be able to meet my daughter everyday, in addition, I have lost my trust in the court system anyway. I am hoping to find another woman and marry again and have a new family now. My ex has asked me many times to come back, even begged me and has attempted to sexually seduce me many time to go back with her, which I always refuse.

My ex-wife could have been rescued from her violence if the domestic violence 'experts' in Canada were not so out of touch with reality. They wrongfully justified her abuse, and dismissed my problems based on absolutely unacceptable basis of 'cultural background'. They convinced her that she was the abused, and I was the abuser and they convinced me too, practically putting me in danger of suicide and also suffering from sexual impotence, which was in fact panic attack during sex, and general depression. I have forgiven my ex-wife because I believe she is a lost and ignorant individual but I will not forgive the stupidity and prejudice in the court, police, and domestic violence centers in Canada.

When I contacted Canadian authorities about this issue they said because it was more than two years ago nothing can be done about those organizations. It took me at least 4 years to come out of depression, how could I follow up with these issues earlier? Apparently from the point of view of Canadian legal system when a person is depressed and suicidal and hates himself, obviously he does not deserve any support, especially if he is a male from certain cultural backgrounds.

I am writing this because even though those times are behind me, I feel that people must know what happened to me, I would like to remain unidentified.

Message from Eve – Ok, I cried and I mean I really cried when I read this courageous man's story. Thank you so much for sharing this part of your life with us as you have shown that domestic violence/abuse affects men as well as women. You have also revealed a problem with the Canadian law, something that I am hoping to investigate further in the near future. I found loopholes as I journeyed from victim to survivor and this is why I initiated a hopeful change in the laws in the UK to protect future victims of domestic violence/abuse.

I am sending you a great big hug, you are so brave and I smiled when I read how you have moved on with your life. I wish you nothing but happiness and smiles and one day, maybe when you least expect it, you will find your special lady and I pray experience true love.

Eve x

CHAPTER THIRTY ONE

I grew up in a home where I saw too much. Everyday my parents would argue and it usually ended with my poor mum getting a beating.

My mum, Mary always seemed to have a black eye, a busted lip or something and as kids me and my brother Daniel were used to seeing her walk around the house slowly because she was nursing an injury again or she would spend days locked in her bedroom with only my father allowed in. It was only as I got older that I realised why mum was locked away, dad didn't want us seeing the bruises.

My dad was always yelling about one thing or another, my mum always seemed to be crying or walking around with her head down, I hated it, I hated him for what he was doing to her but I was powerless. I tried to step in many times but was either shoved out of the way or told to "fuck off and mind my own business." I can't begin to tell you how hard it was and I remember once being in the kitchen and dad had his hands around mum's throat I wanted to kill him, I wanted to pick up the bread knife that was on the work top and stick it in him hard but I didn't I was too scared.

When I got to 16 I left home, I just couldn't stand it anymore and despite me and my brother pleading with her to leave him she just wouldn't, she couldn't and so on the day of my birthday I packed my things and moved in with a friend and her parents.

I was always worried about my mum but I couldn't cope with everything that was going on and I was happy living with my friend and her parents who never seemed to argue at all. When I got a call from my hysterical brother I knew I had to go back home. Mum was in a bad way this time and my brother had phoned the police who had taken dad away, I was relieved.

I will never forget what my mum looked like that day when I went to the hospital and for the rest of my life I will feel guilty because I left her. Her face was unrecognisable, her arm and leg in plaster. He had stamped on her repeatedly and she had suffered internal bleeding and so had to have an emergency operation to save her life. I hated my dad and never wanted to see him again.

My mum came home and me and my brother looked after her and even though it took years she got her life back.

Three years ago I met a wonderful man but my mum didn't like him from the start, yep he was an abuser too but I couldn't see it and it was only after I found out I was pregnant and he beat the baby out of me that I found the strength to leave.

I was five months pregnant and had to give birth to my dead daughter.

Now I know first hand what my mum went through, the pain and heartache. I lost my baby to domestic violence and nearly lost myself but thanks to Eve I am now getting the help I need, THANK YOU for saving me.

Message from Eve – You are a strong woman and so is your mum, you both fought domestic violence and won! YOU ARE FREE! Thank you for allowing me to be your friend and I am so glad that you sought the help that you needed. No one has to be alone, no one has to endure violence – there is help out there. As every day passes you will become stronger and please know I am here for you. Stay safe and keep smiling. Your friend Eve x

CHAPTER THIRTY TWO

CHOICE: The Greatest Power We Have By Jill

"I'm not happy. You don't make me happy anymore," my husband blurted as I sank into the sofa next to him one summer evening. "I think I'll be happier without you." It wasn't the first time Harold* said this, or even the tenth. Each time, he insisted I was defective, that I needed to fix myself. He tried to convince me that I didn't really love him and that my biggest problem was not showing him unconditional love. This time I wasn't buying it. I had been on that merry-go-round for almost 25 years. It was time to get off. Harold's happiness was not my responsibility. I exhausted myself trying to remain sane and constantly on guard against his verbal tirades, emotional roller coasters, and attempts to sabotage my joy and suck the life out of me. This was not a healthy relationship. "Do what you have to do," I told him. He left to be with a woman he met in a Christian chat room.

Harold and I had survived monumental challenges during our marriage. Crippling sickness. Abortion. Unemployment and economical hardship. Teenage pregnancy. Incarceration. Sexual molestation of our children by a church member. Natural disasters. Traumatic deaths, including our infant grandson. Drug addiction. Homelessness. Infidelity. Through it all, God was faithful. His mercies were new every morning and His grace was abundant. But mental illness remained constant, like the irritating tag on the neckline of a new shirt.

Depression and emotional instability plagued Harold for years. I suspected he was bipolar like some of his family members, but he resisted getting help (even refused to go when his primary doctor referred him to a psychiatrist for an evaluation). When he was up, life was good. But, just as I felt like I had caught my breath and the kids were relaxed and being themselves again, gloom started creeping in. The crash was coming. I couldn't prevent it. The dark episodes intensified, imposed more often and stuck around like a guest who'd worn out his welcome.

I firmly believe that a person's level of happiness originates in the mind, directly related to thought patterns and attitudes. Genuine happiness is a matter of perspective. Contentment and an overall state of well-being generate joy and peace within a person. Personal peace is freedom from disquieting or oppressive thoughts or emotions, or a state of tranquility or quiet. Emotional turbulence and anxious thoughts disrupt inner harmony by creating stress in the physical body.

If he had a bad day at work, Harold wasn't happy. If he didn't like what was for dinner, Harold wasn't happy. If the weather was too hot or cold or rainy, Harold wasn't happy. If there was no fun money, the whole weekend was ruined. If the kids bickered or needed help with homework, they'd better steer clear of dear old dad; or they'd get blamed for his crappy night off. Our family became conditioned over the years to do everything possible to maintain an acceptable atmosphere in our home or be the perfect family in public, at church or when visiting friends. All just to keep Harold from getting angry and fault us for his discontent. I was the ringmaster and Harold was the audience in the three ring circus of our lives.

It got harder and harder for the children and me to recover and maintain. Harold's capacity to blame and inflame was relentless. It poisoned our marriage and family, and began spilling over onto our neighbors and friends. Once, when Harold had an argument with some longtime friends visiting our home, he forbade our whole family from communicating with them, including their children. It was devastating, especially to the girls, because they had grown up together and were the best of friends. A year and a half later, even though Harold had instigated the argument and justified remaining offended, the wife stopped by and apologized. That day, grace and mercy triumphed. Over the years, small, stinging jibes had grown into full-on verbal cuts that were justified with phrases such as, "Can't you take a joke?" and "Don't be so sensitive." Love pokes had turned into hard pinches and frog-knuckle jabs. "That didn't hurt. I barely touched you." Bruises lasted for days, explained away as "just playing around." Tickle sessions inevitably went too far, with at least one child hurt and crying, told to stop being a baby and sent to another room. Repeated pleas to stop or let go were ignored. Sometimes Harold caught me by surprise; I could not get out of his wrestling holds no matter what I did. He never believed that he was being too rough physically or saw the emotional pain it caused. I still experience temporary paralysis in my face due to a head injury I suffered in one of those unwelcome wrestling matches. Dejected, the children's trust in their father eroded. Dishonored and devalued, my respect for him dwindled. Not a quitter, I clung to faith and hope in God and His ability to make things better.

As the years passed, the less I could protect our children or work toward repairing the damage. Any attempts by me to help Harold understand that his behavior was disrespectful and wounded them was countered with the attitude that he was teaching them to be tough, because he wasn't going to live with a bunch of sissies. Many times I reminded him that expecting to be treated with kindness and gentleness is not being a sissy, and that knowing when to walk away showed good character. Our four daughters and son buried their anger and hardened their hearts even more. To Harold, my advocacy for our children's well-being was treachery. Standing up for one's convictions and morals and thinking for oneself were considered rebellion. Traitors were dealt with harshly. Compliance and unquestioned obedience were rewarded. Controlling his castle and its inhabitants was Harold's way of preserving his illusion and avoiding being alone or taking care of himself. Ashamed, my fear of failure and aversion to confrontation reinforced the walls around us. My safety zone continued to shrink along with my self- respect.

Like peace and joy, safety is integral to mental, emotional and physical well-being. Feeling safe and being secure are similar, but feelings are fickle; they change frequently. Emotional and physical security are two very different conditions, yet they are interdependent. Predictable situations or behaviors do not guarantee safety or security. Stability is what we actually seek. But, we settle for predictable and the illusion of safety or happiness even if it is only temporary. The intense longing for "safe" pushes us to accept situations that don't serve us. Maintaining the illusion usually limits the experience of the very well-being we seek. At this point, we have betrayed ourselves.

After Harold's 'mistake' (as he called it), I agreed to give him one more chance and work at repairing our relationship. We were still married, but I lived in despair. I loved Harold by choice. Love doesn't fail, I told myself. Love believes and hopes. Love bears all things and doesn't give up. Love forgives and holds no record of wrongs. I thought if I loved Harold enough, was patient and showed him

kindness, even when he spit in my face, pulled my hair (or worse) or called me derogatory names, I believed love would triumph. I was almost emotionally dead, mentally and physically damaged, and spiritually suffocating. God's precious gifts of life and time had been squandered on preserving the illusion. The reality was that I had painfully, slowly lost my personhood and our marriage was suffering an agonizing death. It had been on life support too long.

I tried desperately to please Harold, and I was miserable. Politely addressing issues just made things worse. Harold didn't want to grow up or take responsibility for the messes he made in his life. Mostly, he wanted me to not rock the boat. That meant I was expected to accept his philandering, never disagree with him about anything, and be available at his convenience-physically, emotionally, mentally, and financially. Deep down, I knew that real love did not require me to participate in activities or allow behaviors that went against my basic values and beliefs. I didn't know how, but this madness had to stop. I was done pretending to be someone I wasn't, trying to change myself to please Harold. I was done compromising my values and beliefs in order to avoid his wrath. I decided that I had to change for myself. I prayed for the courage to see the truth, let grace do its work in me and free me from the agony that I could no longer hide. I asked the Lord to show me what to stand for and how.

Maturity is the ability to see and accept truth and reality. Perceiving reality is essential to the healing process. The more we heal, the clearer reality becomes to us. Healing frees us from the pain and wounds of our afflictions, and we feel safe. Emotional maturity insists that we commit ourselves to find safety in the truth. When we know the truth, it will set us free.

Determined to find the truth, I gave permission to what was deepest in me to come out and take its place. I wanted to identify the origins of the wounds, face the pain, and begin a new healing journey. For the next year, I quietly read, researched and digested childhood abuse and how it breeds behaviors in us. Awareness and insight led me to seek information about abuse in adult relationships. Knowledge, understanding and models for addressing destructive patterns of behavior empowered me to take the first steps toward freedom from abuse.

I decided to take a stand for the truth. No more lies. No more half-truths. I began to discover my true self, the person I am beyond the fear. With resolve, I began resisting Harold's attempts to control my thoughts, emotions and vocabulary. I practiced being civil. I refused to be servile. "You're not a good wife! You don't love me!" He thought I was being defiant and told me so with words like contentious, rebellious, unsubmissive, selfish, and stubborn. In an all-out rage, he would spew a string of degrading words at me a sailor would be ashamed to say. I was learning when to say no to something I knew wasn't good for me.

This was definitely not the marriage I wanted or hoped for twenty-five years ago when I said, "I do." I finally accepted that my husband was incapable and unwilling to be faithful to me the day I discovered the engagement ring he bought. It was almost Christmas. Harold said it was meant to be a surprise. Disappointed that he didn't even get me a card for our 25th anniversary two months earlier, I thought maybe he had decided to really commit himself to our relationship. I was a little skeptical, and I didn't trust him. Sure enough, the marriage proposal and honey-dripping messages in Harold's cell phone were not sent to me. I had been played like a ragtime piano.

"Happily ever after" was a dream shattered many times over. Broken vows, broken hearts, broken lives. Attempts at restoring them were beyond hope now. Abuse permeated every area of the relationship. What I had was not a marriage. It was a prison sentence. The truth was that I couldn't have the marriage or the life I wanted. I began asking God to help me to know what it is that He wants me to have, and how to get it.

The ability to choose is the greatest power within a person. Understanding the power of choice is paramount to victorious living. We were created with the freedom to think and to act. The choices we make and how we move forward (or not) are up to us. We must grow up, show up, and take responsibility for our actions. The past is the past and cannot be changed or replaced. The good news is, each person has control over his or her future and the choices ahead.

I couldn't hold it in any longer. I was desperate. I needed someone to talk to. I needed to know my options and my rights. I sought help and found a female Christian counselor. I broke the silence. We talked, texted, met together, prayed. She taught me that acting in my own best interest and taking care of myself is not selfishness. I also learned that submissive is not being passive and self-degrading. I came to understand that Harold's lack of self-control was his problem and not my fault (as he had convinced me to believe). I was off the merry-go-round, but it was time to leave the park.

Remain calm and prepare carefully, the counselor told me. Maintain routines, but don't lose ground. Speak up; voice your disapproval of certain behaviors. Communicate what will no longer be tolerated and the actions you will take if a line is crossed. One of the lines was physical violence. I told Harold if he touched me in anger again, in any way that wasn't gentle and loving; I would leave, call the police, and divorce him. This was his last chance. Was it difficult? you ask. Absolutely! But, I had peace. For the first time, I had support I could trust. Most importantly, I had my Lifeline.

The more Harold tried to hold the illusion together and avoid responsibility for his actions, the less self-control he had. Rarely did he have an 'up' day anymore. I stood firm and prayed for courage to speak the truth. One night, Harold flew into a rage because I didn't agree to let him borrow my car to go visit "a friend" who lived several hundred miles away. Eyes bulging, he grabbed me by my shirt collar, his knuckles digging into my throat, and threatened to kill me if I ever referred to his friendship with that woman as adultery again. Out of the heart the mouth speaks. I believed him.

Proverbs 27:12 says, "The prudent see danger and seek refuge, but the simple keep going and suffer for it." I had lived in danger for a long time. I kept going, and I suffered for it. My children had suffered. My family and friends had suffered. My jobs had suffered. Now life and death had been set before me. I chose life. My life. A life free from abuse. After my shift ended the next day, I went home and loaded my escape bag and a few more things I needed for work in my car. I drove to the local refuge for victims of domestic abuse, where I lived in safety while I made other changes in my life. I got a protective order against Harold. A women's legal advocacy organization assisted me with filing for divorce and navigating the court system.

My hope and belief that Harold would return to his charming self and once again be a man who lived to love and serve God rather than himself was terribly hard to give up. Just as heart-wrenching was letting go of what I'd imagined our life would be. The man he promised to be at the altar never existed. What hurt the most was the revelation that the love of my life never really loved me. It only felt like love to Harold because he didn't know who he was without me. From the very beginning, he convinced me that he needed me (and that I needed him somehow) and he called it love.

I forgave Harold for what he did to me, my dream and our marriage. I forgave myself for enabling him and allowing the abuse. I also forgave myself for the things I did that hurt Harold. I know now that forgiveness doesn't say its okay that someone hurt me or that I hurt someone (intentionally or not). Forgiveness says that I'm okay with moving on and releases me to be free to truly love. The cycle of pain and abuse in my family, in my marriage, and in my life had to stop. Its end began when I stopped betraying myself.

I took the one part of me Harold hadn't destroyed-my faith-and I am rebuilding my life without him. One day at a time, I lean on the Lord; I don't attempt to understand everything anymore. I trust that God will keep His promises to me, and I look to Him for answers. I praise and thank Jesus for the peace He sends and for His unconditional love. I know the problems ahead of me will never be stronger than the power behind me when I lean on the Lord. My recovery journey continues. Sometimes bittersweet, but peace, joy and the freedom to be myself are great rewards.

Recently, Harold telephoned me. We hadn't spoken for a year. After some small talk about family matters, he apologized for the mess he'd made in our marriage and for hurting me. I accepted his apology. Then he told me he was miserable and didn't think he would ever be happy without me. "I'm happy without you, Harold," I replied. "It's time you moved on. The choice is yours."

*Harold is not his real name.

Message from Eve – Wow! This brought back so many memories for me, walking on eggshells was a specialty of mine. I'm so happy you are free and a big thank you for sharing. Survivors not victims! Eve x

CHAPTER THIRTY THREE

They say it is a cycle. They tell the truth. Sometimes mothers protect their daughters from the ugly raw truth of their fathers, they hope to spare them the anguish that he is really a monster.

My mom did this to protect me I know but instead I never knew the things that were not normal in a relationship. I thought it was our job as wives to do anything our husbands wanted. I as a mother protected, or so I thought my daughter.

I explained away his behavior I did not want her to see. She still does not know it all; I can not bear to tell her.

She is in her twenties now and I could not hide it all. This is for her and her sister and all the young ladies I hope to reach. It is also for the moms who with our protective instincts are only harming our children by not telling them what to avoid and how to protect themselves.

I met him at 16, I thought it was love. He was 32. I saw him first at a family friend's home and then I skipped school to see him as the school had no way to contact my parents. I left home in the middle of the night at 17 to be with him. He seemed a dream to a young girl who grew up with no money and was from a drug home. He bought me things and told me he loved me. I graduated high school and left with him.

I got pregnant and married him because I was taught that is how it is. I still was on a cloud, in love. During this time he began to tell me that the people who talked to me or that I knew just wanted me for sex, this was the beginning of the verbal abuse.

I had a beautiful baby girl and I hoped he would be happy having a family and stop the abuse. We lived in a trailer at the time and I couldn't go outside with my daughter cause someone would hit up on me, he said. It was so hard not to be like the other moms and take my child out into the sunshine. I did as he asked.

As I write this I am sickened cause I did not see.

He then got a job in Louisiana so we moved there. This is when the physical abuse began. I will keep it short cause the memories are to deep.

We both worked in the telemarketing room, I did the paperwork. He said that day that one of our delivery drivers hit up on me, none of them did. I told him that and when we went home that evening he started again telling me one of them had. He held me up against the wall off the floor while he beat me in the rib all the while telling me I was trash and a slut. I was never away from him and the only time we had someone else was when he wanted it.

It was here that I learned that if you scream for help that no one will come.

We were only there a short time after that, he lost the job.

We then moved home to the small town where we were from and he started working as a restaurant assistant manager. We lived in a trailer again and I still could not go outside when he was gone or he would tell me I was seeing other people.

I hid from the world.

He wanted other girls and I gave him what he wanted. I later found out that one of them was a revenge thing on his part cause her boyfriend liked me. I never knew. No one, even family, could come see my daughter and I if he was not home, he said everyone wanted something from me.

It's hard to remember all the details but we fought all the time and things were broken, I lived for my daughter and hoped that one day he would stop.

Time passed with our daughter growing. We saw family when he permitted it and he would always tell me I came from a bad family. I prayed for guidance. I was pushed around but the mental abuse was eating at me and there was no way to please him.

We moved to a bigger town and it was hard. We lived in a hotel for awhile but finally we got a house. Our daughter started school and that is when he decided we had to do meth. I by this time would do as he asked because then he was not as abusive. I did not understand that him harassing me into drugs was abuse. I decided maybe if I started college it might help and so I went to talk to the college adviser, a guy who hit up on me. My husband told me it was my fault if anyone hit up on me and he decided no college. It hurt; he harassed me and said such awful things to me that I gave up on the hope for college.

We moved across town later, a better school for our daughter, she never complained. She was a quiet child, in pain from all the fighting. I was a young mom; I had no idea the pain in her from seeing the fights.

While there, at our new home, many things happened, it was chaos. Fighting and we had problems paying rent so I convinced him to let me work part time at the school in the lunchroom. All the staff were women but one. He constantly harassed me about his belief that the one man there was sleeping with me but we needed the money.

Years passed during which the abuse continued. I was dragged through the car by my hair. I watched my child be carried up the street screaming for me cause he said he was taking her away because I was seeing other people. He told me no one would ever want me. He tried to stab me in the throat with the vacuum cleaner; I dodged and took it in the shoulder. Our daughter screamed "please don't hurt mommy.'

The fighting was getting worse. My daughter became a young woman and started young woman things. He told her that now she was a woman and would be a slut too, we hated him. He told me that if I left he would take our daughter and he would harm my family. I couldn't be friends with anyone cause they wanted me he said. He was mentally abusive still and occasionally physically abusive.

I wound up pregnant in 2003, he said it had to be someone else's; I had not been with any other guys in our marriage. I told him this and he called me a liar.

The fighting was everyday now. Our oldest child had become a recluse in her room. She was 12.

I wound up having a girl; she was born 3 weeks early. I felt something was wrong that day with the baby. I told him and we went to the hospital. Her cord was wrapped around her neck and arm, and her breathing was stopping and then starting. They induced labor. When born she was a premiee, her weight was high for one but she had to be under a lamp.

The hospital was suspicious of him, he had upset me so bad that it had upset the baby in me. They kept asking if I even wanted him to be there, I knew better than to say no.

After that he lightened up some but then started again.

I left last year. I was having panic attacks but I thought it was heart attacks. I went to the doctor and he told me I needed to get away from what was causing them.

I would lie on the floor in a ball holding myself, trying to block out his words, he would stand over me, in front of our children and say them anyway.

Our youngest was peeing her pants when she was home, her grades were failing in school, it was too much for her. I am not sure how her sister lived through it all but I saw the signs in our youngest daughter and it scared me.

Then one afternoon he got mad at our oldest daughter. He picked up a child's chair to hit her with it, I jumped in between. I knew the time to go had come and so I started planning.

I had my brother come get me, he helped me escape.

I lost most of what I owned, so did our children. We have moved everywhere to hide.

He started ' Hit No More 'classes so I moved in with his cousin and him. The abuse started again and he stopped his classes. I went to a domestic violence Shelter; it was life changing. When I got out I moved in with a friend but she let him move in, I had nowhere to go.

He harassed me into giving him what he wanted and I wound up pregnant. I miscarried' the baby was 10 weeks along. I was shattered that a baby died in me. He used it to abuse me further, he said I killed our baby, I did not. I was 39 when I got pregnant. I am not sure what caused the miscarriage.

I moved in with family.

I have recently learned he did this to his past wives. I still have nightmares of him coming to get me, our daughters do too. Sometimes people say things that sound like him, when this happens I get sad and hurt so bad and the dreams are horrid. His words haunt me; I pray they will go away someday, I can only imagine the nightmares in my daughter's minds. That makes me sad.

You are asking why did I stay 20 years, I was so scared he would carry out his threats of killing my family and taking my children, see children have no say if they don't want to see a parent. Our youngest has no choice, the courts and Judges did not see their mommy on the floor having a major panic attack or their mommy being hit.

Our children were terrorized and they have to see the attacker. It is so sad. Currently our oldest child, now 21 has married. Her husband is amazing to her. I am so happy she did not find someone like her father.

Her father sends her constant threats on text and voicemail. Our youngest still has nightmares and she sees a counselor. She is afraid daddy will come take her from me. She says she hates him for what he has done. I am filing for divorce and he is hiding so I can't have the divorce papers served. I had to change my number, he texted and said he was going to our daughter's school and moms and kids would be hurt by the guns he was bringing, he then said he will shoot me. It is on voicemail as well and I have a restraining order against him. I do not know where he is but he does know where I am. He has not even written to his daughter.

Message from Eve – Brave, brave lady. I am pleased to hear that your eldest daughter has gone on to find a nice, young man. I hope you and your daughter's find peace and please know that I am here for you whenever you need to chat. Eve x

CHAPTER THIRTY FOUR

Did I ever love him, I don't know. He was nice enough at first I suppose but whenever his mates were around he would always poke fun at me, I guess he thought it made him look cool.

He was hot and the sex was always good, he taught me so many things but by the age of 18 he'd convinced me that sleeping with other men for money was a good and easy way to make money and so he became my pimp. Every night I would kiss him goodbye and get in the car of some stranger, he set the meetings up and bought me new clothes and sexy lingerie so I looked good for the "clients." I always left with a bag of sniff to help me get through the night, Malcolm said it was a good way of blocking it all out and making sure I had fun and pleased the punters.

It was kinda fun and I liked going to the restaurants and swanky hotels. I was what Malcolm called a "top piece of ass" and he charged the men a fortune for one night with me, good job because my cocaine habit was spiralling out of control, I needed shit loads to even put a smile on my face.

One morning I woke up and had a really bad migraine, I begged Malcolm to cancel that night but he said we really needed the money, he promised we were going to move abroad as soon as we made enough money and so struggling out of bed I forced myself to get showered and dressed in time for Mr Duncan.

Clive arrived at the usual time, I had been seeing him regularly for the last 8 months and he was a sweet man with a bad stammer but we always had a good time. We hadn't had sex that often, Clive preferred to talk instead.

I can't really talk much about what happened that night but I spent over four weeks recovering in the hospital and now have a very large scar that runs down the side of my face, I'm also permanently deaf in one ear from the blows to the side of my head. Clive wasn't a sweet man he was a violent monster who kept me captive for 2 days whilst he raped me not only himself but with a variety of objects and beat me. He also anally raped me.

I gave the cops a statement but I knew what they were thinking I deserved it; I was a prostitute after all. Clive hung himself before he was arrested so I will never get the justice I deserved.

Malcolm looked after me after the accident until I was well again, he said I couldn't go back to the way I worked before and so within weeks I was on the streets prostituting my body, I couldn't get any lower. I hated doing it but if I didn't then Malcolm wouldn't let me have the drugs I so badly needed, I was hooked and trapped.

I didn't make much money, my ugly face put the punters off and Malcolm was beating me more and more. His words really hurt me too, I had always done everything he wanted, I had even broken the law but now I was broken he no longer wanted me.

I remember crying, I didn't want to be on my own and so he said he would stay, this is when my hell really started.

For the next year I was raped, beaten and basically used as a piece of meat by Malcolm and his friend, he said where, he said when. I could be fast asleep in bed and they would come bursting in, do what they had to do then they would leave. I was addicted to any drug I could get my hands on.

I finally ran away and went back home to my mom and dad. Things aren't good between us but I'm working on it, I'm working on me. I go to therapy every week and have started night classes. People stare at me but I'm kinda used to it now. Then I met this wonderful lady Eve on Facebook and my life suddenly changed, I'm not a victim anymore I'm a survivor. I still find it really hard to look at myself in the mirror but Eve has encouraged me to look deeper to search within myself as she says and I'm slowly finding the real me and realizing it doesn't matter what is on the outside it's what's in a person's heart that matters.

Message from Eve – I knew you could do it! Go you! Since we began talking you have blossomed and become so much stronger. There is life after domestic violence and rape YOU CAN DO IT! I'm so proud! Your friend. Eve x

CHAPTER THIRTY FIVE

I had been reading 50 Shades of Grey, I hadn't got very far, I think it was the main characters first meeting or maybe when he came to the store, her place of work and purchased cable ties. I triggered. I have since learnt what a "trigger" is, I do it often and I have learned coping techniques.

I had my own Grey but unlike Ana in the book I wasn't a virgin and he wasn't my first love, I had not long divorced and I had a young child.

When he came into my life it would never be the same again. My self esteem was low and I was extremely flattered by his attention, his full on attention. He was strong, determined and he knew what he wanted in life, he wanted me. When he wasn't with me he was calling, texting, emailing or chatting to me online.

When he was able to be with me there wasn't time for anyone else, we couldn't get enough of each other. I was obsessed! The sex was intense but unlike Ana it was me who got the handcuffs out, it was me who suggested different things. I was turning him on and it was an aphrodisiac.

I had always been rubbish at decision making, no problem my Grey liked to make the decisions; he had it all in hand. To top it all he was great with my son too.

So what's not to like you may ask? Lucky girl you say. He was hot and after the rejection of my first husband, when he asked me to move half way across the country to be with him, why on earth would I say no? Are you crazy?

Within 6 months I had moved in with my son, my new life, new man and a new start but I missed something out. You see in hindsight I can look back and see the red flags, those warning signs that were there from the start.

Around 6 weeks before I moved in with him I went out with a friend, we went clubbing. He wasn't happy about me going out but instead of telling me I couldn't he went round to his ex girlfriends for the evening. The texts were continual, my friend told me to put the phone away, I was with her, not him. I did. When I got back to my phone he had gone mad, he was fuming that I had stopped responding to texts. He had a good mind to come down there and get me (250 miles.) he said. I didn't go clubbing again.

You very quickly learn not to do the things that make them angry. He was worried about me; anything could have happened to me, his panic was his lack of control from so far away, I know that now.

So lets roll this forward to 8 years later!

Friends had gradually faded away, we had children together. I received a phone call from my ex husband "Your parents are worried about you and him." I told him they were paranoid. "Has he ever hit you?" My reply "Oh come on, he would never hit me, he's a great man." "What's he like with my child?" "Listen he's a great dad, he would never hurt any of us, he loves us."

But he had hurt my eldest, I didn't say that because I honestly believed at the time he had done it for his own good, my son was extremely well behaved and I believed it was because he had a firm hand with him.

So 8 years in I was convincing others everything was ok. I actually was not convinced myself. I was convinced he would not harm us but he was moody and I wasn't pleasing him sexually anymore and well I don't know, however hard I tried I just couldn't get things right. I was always walking on eggshells trying not to set him off.

Then it happened. A moment in my life when I realised he viewed me and the children as possessions and not human beings, not people, not individuals with opinions of their own, just extensions of himself. I never saw it coming, I should have.

Now I stumble with my words when it has been pretty free flowing up to now, that moment of realisation when your dreams come crashing down and you are trapped, you are incapable of keeping your children safe and your friends have all but given up on you. I was well and truly isolated and it turns out the people I did confide in were not to be trusted.

My life was a living hell and I had walked into there freely, my own choice, consensual, if only I had known! I spent nearly 2 years trapped, too scared to leave, petrified that if I stayed I could be dead in a moment. Do you realise the damage that does to your children? When your child hold his mobile phone in bed for hours not knowing when to dial 999, not knowing if he would get in trouble for calling the police, when all your son wants to do is grow up so he is big enough to take on his step father.

A character just like Christian Grey was my husband, he is now my ex husband. It's all about control and power.

Message from Eve – I am so happy that you are happy and free at last and that your children are too. May your smiles continue. Eve x

CHAPTER THIRTY SIX

I write this letter to you as part of my recovery, as part of the healing process that I am having to go through because of you.

I write you this letter because I need answers. What did I ever do wrong? What did I ever do to you other than love you?

Was it so wrong to be a woman? Was it such a crime to want to be a woman, act like a woman, be treated like a woman? Was it so wrong to want to be loved and cherished, to be adored as I adored you?

You always used to say that I provoked you, I really did try my best to please you but somehow it never was good enough for you. I tried so hard, I really did and no matter how many times I got it wrong I still tried so hard to please you.

When you hit me you hurt me but when you raped me I died. I felt numb.

I said no to you that first time so many times and I begged you to stop but you wouldn't, why wouldn't you stop? Why did you want to hurt me so bad? With every tear and cry you hurt me more. I will never be able to forget that look on your face as you rammed yourself into me and caused me so much pain, I will never forget your eyes, you are evil.

For years you abused me you abused my body but my body will heal, my brain, my mind I don't know, is it even possible? You created so much hurt, so many scars when you abused me the way you did.

Yes I went to the police and had you arrested and now you sit in your jail cell with lots of time to think. Do you ever think about what you did to me, what you put me through or do you still not care? You have probably forgotten about me.

My healing has begun and I know I am going to get better, stronger you will always be the low life scumbag you have always been and I'm thankful for the chance to be able to write you this letter and tell you exactly how I feel. I hate you and I have never hated anyone in my entire life so you get it all, the lot!

You took away my innocence, my life with your threats and demands and violence well I've got it back and I just want to say I AM GLAD YOU ARE IN JAIL, I AM GLAD I WAS STRONG ENOUGH TO ESCAPE but what I really want to say is FUCK YOU!

I think I'm gonna keep writing these letters because they empower me even more, make me feel strong and every day I feel myself heal just a little bit more. I know I won't mail them but then maybe one day I will but for now I want to say it again FUCK YOU!

From

Louise The Survivor!

Message from Eve – Stay strong, stay empowered but most of all stay safe. When I suggested you write these letters to your abuser to empower yourself and clear your mind I had a feeling they would help. Your voice, never to be silenced. Eve x

CHAPTER THIRTY SEVEN

I was pregnant with our third baby when he beat me for the last time and for the last four years I've lived as an almost recluse.

We moved to Australia ten years ago, I didn't want to go but it was supposed to be a fresh start for us, he promised that the violence would end but it never did.

I was a very lively teenager who loved to party but worked hard through university and then medical school and when I met David I knew that he would be the only man I ever loved.

When he hit me for the first time I knew it was my fault, I answered him back and as the argument went on I just wouldn't back down, I tormented him I guess, I pushed him over the edge but the slap to the face would have been enough, the broken wrist was a step too far but I forgave him after all it was my fault.

In 2002 I'd had enough and I told him. He pleaded with me to stay and that's when we started to talk about moving to Australia. My parents no longer talked to me, they didn't like the bruises and the fact that I always went back but it was my life and so I agreed to emigrate.

It was really easy for me to get a job and within two weeks of landing in Melbourne I was working in the hospital and began to make new friends, I was happy, David was happy and within a few months I was pregnant.

I never went back to work, I couldn't David wanted me to stay home and so before I knew it I was a full time mum. I love my children very much but I missed work, I missed the thrill of saving a stranger's life and the buzz of a hospital environment, I was lonely.

David lost his job as I found out I was pregnant with our third child and that is when everything fell apart.

The violence began to escalate and he never seemed to have a nice word to say to anyone even to the kids. I was 24 weeks pregnant when David almost killed me and my unborn child.

Waking in the middle of the night with cramp I hobbled around the bedroom trying to ease the pain. I was being as quiet as possible because I knew how grouchy he could be if woken up. I stubbed my toe on the dresser which woke him and the next minute he grabbed me by the hair throwing me on the bed. I don't know how long it took him to punch me unconscious but my nose and mouth were bleeding profusely and I knew my cheek bone was smashed before it all went black. When I woke up David was nowhere to be seen, all I could see was blood and I was in labour.

My third baby, a little girl who I named Lucy died inside my womb and along with her a very big part of me died also.

I cry every day and I don't sleep well; I merely carry on breathing for my two children.

I don't like going out, I have no friends and when I came across Eve Thomas's website after finding her on Facebook I reached out after I read a message she had posted. I'm now not lonely. Eve guided me in the right direction and I made contact with Lifeline Australia and I am getting better, I've even been out. I'm stuck in Australia with no way of getting back home yet but who knows maybe one day.

I know I will never be the person I was before but for me and my children life is now peaceful, no more shouting, no more violence.

Message from Eve – Thank you so much for reaching out, no one ever should be alone! I have cried so much whilst reading all the stories I have received but yours really got to me. I am so happy you are venturing out and have made new friends and I wish all the luck and happiness in the world for you and your children. You have a friend. Eve x

CHAPTER THIRTY EIGHT

My name is Hope and I was a victim of brutal domestic abuse. I am telling my story simply to help millions of women who are still in such relationships. I do not tell this story to pull at your heart strings or as a stereotype but I tell this story to create awareness, to let people know that these things are happening. I have requested my real identity be kept a secret because I am still in my transition process, I am sure with time I will be able to reveal my identity.

I was married for 9 years and I have 2 kids, both girls. I endured abuse for 7 years out of those 9 years. My second child suffers from brain damage because when I was 7 months pregnant with her my ex husband pushed me face first into a brick wall, pulled me to the ground and kicked me until I bled, he rushed me to the hospital and the child was brought out immediately, she spent an additional 5 months in the incubator.

I don't know why he did all he did to me but all I know is he did all he did to me and he has no remorse and why should he have any when we live in a country that really has no laws on things like this or even regard women as humans or partners in the home. I live in Nigeria.

He put me through hell for 7 years I cried, I begged and even prayed for death but none of those things helped me. Rape was a norm for me and at a point I would just close my eyes and wait until he was done, I stopped feeling anything for him so I became a zombie. Nothing I ever did made him happy so I stopped trying and just kept doing what I did. It didn't matter if the house was spotless or filthy I still got the same reaction. Beating me up was like a drug for him, I would see him restless for hours until he laid hands on me then he would relax and even venture a smile.

If he got heat from work he would unload on me, if he had money problems, you guessed it; somehow I would be the one wasting all his money. He beat me up for having girls, he beat me up for looking at him funny, he beat me up for singing or breathing, in short he beat me for being alive.

I reported him to the police several times but the response was always the same. "Madam, it is a family issue and you need to work it out with your husband."

I tried to leave several times but just as I was about to leave I would stop and look at my kids. I had nothing, no source of income, no place to go, nothing and my second child required constant medical attention and so with those thought I would shelve the idea of an escape and convince myself I was staying for my children.

What changed?

On this faithful night when he came home he was not particularly angry but I felt very uneasy, I knew a storm was brewing so I just braced myself for the worst. Not long after I put the kids to sleep he summoned me to his room, he was sitting on a stool with a bottle of vodka in his hands. He ordered me to close the door and strip well like I stated earlier this was routine to me so I just went through the motions. I took off all my clothes and preceded to the bed, I knew the drill. I lay on the bed and spread my legs; he took a long gulp and dropped the bottle. He took off his shorts and climbed on top of me. He spread my legs with so much aggression and proceeded to penetrate me and suddenly he flew into a rage and hit me across the face calling me a prostitute, he said I was giving my body out to other men so much and that I had gotten so used to them that this caused me not to get wet enough for him to penetrate and in the process bruised himself. He never considered the pain I felt each he penetrated me, it was like having a baby every time, the pain was so intense I would sit in hot water for hours just to get over the soreness.

He pulled me up, pulled out a belt and proceeded to beat me like a mule; he tied me to the chair and flogged me like I was some slave. I closed my eyes and bit my lip so I wouldn't scream. He called me all sorts of names but one statement he made would change my life forever, "You are a worthless being, you were born worthless and you will die worthless, I own you and your forsaken children. You can't even produce useful children, you are worse than an animal."

That night I decided enough was enough, he continued to flog me until his hands got weak and he kicked me out of his room naked and bleeding. I whispered a thank you and walked into the bathroom and for the first time in 7 years I did not cry. That night I realized I needed to hear all that to wake me up, I suddenly realized that it couldn't be as bad out there as it was in here so I decided I was walking away with my girls and I was not going to look back.

The next morning after he left for work I went into his room, searched and found some money. I packed light and took the girls and we left. I travelled back to my home town, I had an aunt whom I knew from childhood and I hoped she was still alive, I guess the universe was on my side because she was. When I got there I narrated everything to her, she wept and wept some more.

I left my girls with her with a little money; she assured me some natural herbs would be used for my second daughter. I came back to town and got a job as a cleaner at the cinema, it helps me keep a low profile, people usually don't notice cleaners.

Long story short, I went through hell. I left because I realized I wasn't worthless. I suddenly realised I wasn't property to be owned, I realized I was of better use to my children alive than dead. I doubt if I would ever have a meaningful relationship with any other human, I seriously have trust issues but I am here to tell you what no book, blog or psychiatrist will tell you, the decision to leave an abusive relationship lies totally in your hands so decide now and decide fast. My name is Hope and I survived.

Message from Eve – Hope's story was shared by a GENTLEman who lives in Nigeria and works tirelessly as he campaigns against domestic violence and rape. Arome Ameh has kindly agreed to be #OneVoice's ears and eyes in Nigeria and together we are working to set up a trust which will be governed in the UK by a board of trustees. The Nigerian trust will receive a 1/50 share of the total revenue of this book and The Eve Thomas Foundation will ensure that every penny is used to help Nigeria's victims. Eve x

CHAPTER THIRTY NINE

I met my abuser through Facebook we chatted for about 6 months then decided to meet up one day. We went for a walk down the river and sat and just talked for a few hours from there on things moved pretty quickly between us and he almost immediately moved into my house. Things were going good at first but one night because he had no cannabis he started screaming and shouting, throwing things round the house and then he gripped me by the throat and pinned me up against the wall not only to me but my daughter too. He started head butting me and then my daughter he kept saying that one of us was lying, so I said I was lying even though I didn't even know what he was talking about but I wanted him to let go of my daughter so he did and continued to head butt me over and over again. He finally let me go and just went back on his computer like nothing had happened he was always on the computer from when he woke up till he went to sleep.

The day after when I showed him the bruises and what he had done to me he said he couldn't remember anything and I just left it at that as I didn't want him to get angry again.

He would drink everyday and make me to and I wasn't allowed to talk to my family at all as he said they was trying to turn me against him so I had no one to talk to or turn to. My daughter went on a sleep over so he decided he wanted to go out clubbing which I didn't really want to but I did anyway, so we get into the club and he starts talking to a young girl she was only 18 as she told me he was dancing with her and was all over her and I didn't know what to do. He then says to me were taking her home for a 3 some I said no were not and I walked out of the club and started to walk home, then I heard someone was behind me and it was him by himself and very angry. He grabbed my arm and made me walk fast with him and didn't talk to me I was absolutely petrified of what would happen when I got home. When I got home he made me sit on the chair beside him while he was playing on the pc doing some DJ thing. He kept calling me a bitch and I will never find anyone else and he doesn't know why he is with me anyway because I'm not his type. I was just sat crying and didn't say anything was too scared to and then he grabbed me by my hair and he had his penis out and said suck that if you love me and I said no. He forced my head down and made me suck it I was gagging but he had hold of my hair so tight and pushing me onto him I had no choice. When it had all finished he said now get to fucking bed and stay there. When I went to bed I just cried my eyes out for hours and eventually I did fall asleep and was dreading going downstairs in the morning he was lying on the sofa asleep and when I went to make myself a drink he woke up and cuddled me and said what happened last night. I didn't know what to do so I didn't say anything and it was like he was trying to say he didn't know what happened but he did.

My daughter told my family about him hitting her and me so my younger brother informed the police and social services and then he came to my house to check if I was ok, my abuser stuck a knife to my throat and said if you open that door I will kill you, at that moment I actually thought I was going to die, The social services wouldn't let my daughter back in my house till he had gone so the same day he packed his bags and went, I was relieved but also scared that he would come back and hurt me I blocked him on Facebook and I blocked his number on my phone a few weeks went by and I was on my pc reading my emails when I noticed one from him saying he's sorry and won't do it again and could we meet to talk, how stupid of me to agree. I felt really rubbish about myself all my confidence had gone I was a wreck so I basically took him back biggest mistake I could of made. Not only did I have to deal with him but my ex husband was giving me abuse to I was in a living hell I had my ex husband threatening to kill me and one time as I was walking down the street he grabbed me by the throat luckily my brother was there to grab him of me. I got an injunction on him but he still kept harassing me so every time he did I phoned the police and eventually he stopped but now when I look back why the hell did I not report the guy that I was with who was mentally and physically abusing me, Think that was the manipulation I thought I needed him and also scared of the repercussions of what would happen if I told the police. I thought I loved him and thought he loved me well he would tell me he did but looking now you don't hurt people you love,

Things was going good for the next few weeks I just did everything I could to please him and tried not to do anything that would make him angry. He spent all his money on cannabis and beer but also spent the majority of mine on it to and I had a daughter to support but if I didn't give him the money he would start shouting and throwing things round the house, I never had no money and was like a prisoner I couldn't go nowhere only to buy his beer, I started drinking everyday to just to get through and to please him because he said he didn't like drinking on his own, I was sat doing something on my pc which was next to his I got a message of a male on Facebook which was only a friend asking how I was and he saw it he starting saying that I was having an affair he gripped me by my hair and made me sit next to him and not move I was telling him I hadn't done anything its just a message. He started punching me everywhere I begged him to stop but he just wouldn't he kept hitting and hitting I was terrified I curled up in a ball and was crying. Finally he stopped and told me to go to bed which I did I just lay there crying and scared and eventually I fell asleep. The next day I woke up I was covered in bruises from head to toe, he said he couldn't remember doing it he said he must have blacked out as usual he was sorry and things just carried on like it didn't happen.

On the night he had got some cocaine he kept telling me to take some to I said no and was adamant I was not going to do that I don't agree with drugs he was gripping my hair pushing my face into it to try to force me to I just pretended to otherwise I would of got another beating. He run out of cannabis so was pacing the front room and shouting I was sat thinking oh no what's going to happen now he started throwing things round the room big chairs and it nearly hit me, it just smashed into bits he just wouldn't stop shouting he started going through the ashtray to see if he could get any out of the used ones he'd already smoked, so I helped him just so he would calm down but he didn't he was going on and on for hours. Eventually we went to bed he grabbed me put me on all fours and started to put himself in my bum I didn't want him to do it and he was penetrating my bum very hard he had hold of my hair pulling my head backwards and he just kept going till he had finished. I was in pain I went to the bathroom and wiped myself and noticed blood I felt dizzy so lay on the bathroom floor. I stayed there for hours crying and scared I felt disgusted and dirty and I felt sick. I kept asking myself why am I putting up with this I ran a bath and just sat in it washing myself over and over and still I didn't inform the police. He just acted like everything was alright I was dying inside I was at the lowest point in my life and I couldn't see any way out I felt trapped scared and alone. Everyday was the same him playing on the pc and me doing everything to please him while he would call me fat, ugly, worthless and no one else would have me and I believed it too.

My daughter went on a sleep over at her aunts me and him had both been drinking everything seemed ok and all of a sudden he jumped up and started throwing the chair about and banging his head against the wall he was going crazy and saying I'm going to fucking kill you, I was terrified so I ran out that front door in my pajamas, no shoes and I could hear him shouting my name and I kept looking behind me to see if he was coming. I have never ran so fast in my life, I ran to my mums house which is like a 20 min walk I got there in about 10, I was hysterical at this point and my mum was panicking because she didn't know what was going on eventually I told her what's been happening. The next day I get a phone call of the police to come talk to me I said yes apparently he had said that my sister had been with someone else and assaulted him I couldn't believe what I was hearing I told the police what had happened and I'd not seen anything. I was the victim but was made to feel like it was me that had done something wrong I lost faith in the police at that point as I showed them the text he sent me the day after saying he was going to kill me and they just wasn't interested. I'd been through hell and back and when I went back to the house he had smashed it up and so I grabbed some things and never went back. I changed my phone number blocked him on Facebook and changed my email address but he made a fake Facebook in my name added my sister my other one and started with threats so she just blocked the account and told me about it. I didn't hear from him at all after that point a year later I was sat watching TV and my daughter came and sat down next to me and said mum I need to tell you something and will you not be mad at me, I said no I could never be mad at you and what she told me made me sick angry and felt like someone had ripped my heart out and stood all over it, she told me he had felt her down there inappropriately I rang the police straight away and a few days later she was took to a centre to give a statement on a camera. I said I wanted to give a statement too so I did, it was horrible reliving the details but I wanted the police to know what sort of person he was. It took months for the police to find him because the name he had told me wasn't even his real name and I could not believe what I was hearing. It was in the paper an appeal to find him, anyway they finally found him and questioned him and he obviously denied everything. A few months later I got a phone call of the police saying there are not charging him as there's no evidence, but my sister got charged for assaulting him and had to go to court and got 3 yrs probation and if she got into anymore trouble then would have to go to jail! I do not condone what my sister did but she got punished and he got away with everything. It took a long time for me to even feel a bit normal again I had panic attacks and flash backs and I had to support my daughter as what happened to her affected her so badly that she was self harming. My daughter now is so happy and

I'm so proud of her and we have both helped each other through the toughest time in our lives.

Message from Eve – I have so much respect for you and your daughter and I hope that smiles and laughter follow you both around every single day. Thank you for your bravery and for sharing your story. Eve x

CHAPTER FORTY

Do you know what it is like growing up hearing shouting and seeing your dad hit your mum all the time, I can tell you its shit.

I can't really remember a day going by when he wasn't shouting or balling about one thing or another and me my sister and mum had to be very quiet because he didn't like noise of any kind, said it hurt his ears.

There's nothing wrong physically with my dad but there is mentally, he's an abuser and he didn't only hit my mum but me and my sister too.

My childhood was ok at times he used to like taking us out for the day but either me or my sister would end up crying because he'd either given us a tongue lashing or a belt, the belts were his speciality.

As I grew up I hated him more and more and my teenage years were spent trying to defend my mum. I should have been thinking about false tan, hair extensions, boys, make up and shoes you know all the things that a young girl should be thinking of not how can I protect her from him.

He was very violent, I think my mum thought me and my sister didn't see, she tried her best to protect us and would sneak into our rooms or text us to check we were ok after one of his outbursts. I saw a lot, I remember a lot and have nightmares most nights because of it, because of him.

One of my nightmares is really bad, I wake to see a man standing in my room with a balaclava on, I know where this came from, this distant memory.

When I was very young I heard noises in the middle of the night, my mummy was trying to be quiet I could tell, I snuck out of bed and went to her room and saw three men pinning her down, one of those men was my daddy, the other two his brothers, I hate my uncles as much as I hate my dad.

My dad hit me and my sister too, he went to punch my sister in the face because she was ill and hit the wall at the side of her head, I was happy when his hand was bleeding, I wanted to kill him, I hated him so much.

We have all had big bald patches on our heads because of him and my mum is very sick now because of all the beatings.

It took my mum a long time to be strong enough to face life on her own but she isn't alone she has me and my sister and we stick together!

Life was shit but my mum got the balls to take action and we have never looked back. Yes the nightmares still come and I'm now getting help and this lady Eve has helped me so much, she's been a good friend and put me in touch with some other people who are helping me. I don't want a boyfriend yet even though I am now 18 years old I think I will find it very hard to trust but my mum keeps telling me not all men hit, I suppose I should believe her really.

My dad was a coward, a bully and I'm glad he is now in jail. He's tried writing to me but I don't want to know that part of my life is over; my counsellor is teaching me that.

I've watched some horrible stuff, I've seen too much and I know my mum did her best to protect me and try to shield me and my sister from it all but we saw. If you are reading my story and have children please don't stay get help and get safe. I want to tell my mum everything I saw but I can't I know it will upset her and it's now my job to look after her, she's my mum.

Message from Eve – I'm so glad I could help you and be your buddy and I'm glad you are now receiving some help honey. You are a VERY BRAVE YOUNG LADY. I have my own guilt regarding my beautiful daughters and what they witnessed/went through but I hope your mum is doing well. You have ALL my respect, there is life after domestic violence and not all men hit, there are good men, GENTLEmen out there we just have to find them. Here for you always. Eve x

CHAPTER FORTY ONE

Sometimes as a small child my mother would take us to the park. I don't mean in the day time although we did go then too but this was at night time when my father had returned home from the pub raging and drunk. My mother would gather us all up and just walk and walk until she was pretty sure he would be sleeping. When we got home we had to be as quiet as mice for fear of waking him, that would really not be good. At other times when the shouting, throwing, banging and slamming began I would crawl under the dining room table, right to the centre and pull all the chairs tightly around me. I felt protected under there, that table and chairs was my little girl fortress from the storm swirling all around me. I never felt loved or wanted by my father, my sister was 'daddy's favourite' and I was always a 'mummy's girl.' It made sense really, she nurtured me and made me feel wanted, he did not, it was that simple. Also of course he was very scary to a little girl. Sometimes he would come home from drinking and if there wasn't the one specific thing he wanted to eat in the kitchen he would throw every single food item onto the floor, never mind that my mother had several children to feed and little money because it was spent in the pub.

Another time he came home and she had been watching a movie, it was almost at the end and he asked for something, she asked if she could just see the last 5 minutes of the film, so he smashed the light bulb in the ceiling. At other times when he wanted peace and quiet he would turn off the electric at the mains. For me this was hell as I was terrified of the dark. Sometimes I would go and sit on the step outside because the street light was lighter than inside the house.

Sometimes my mother would declare she was leaving and this too terrified me, she never said she was leaving with us, just that she was leaving. A few times she did walk out luckily it was a walk to the local shop and then she came back, but for me the horror of her leaving and being left with this scary, violent man was dreadful. Sometimes I would run and fetch the hairbrush when they had been arguing, the hairbrush felt like my magic tool, as she brushed my hair she would calm down and all the time she brushed my hair she was right there with me, a little girls logic eh! Obviously I knew that all of this had been a really unpleasant experience for a little girl but even I shocked myself when twenty plus years on I painted the picture that is included on this blog on my website during an art therapy session. For me the painting was the most poignant message from my inner child that growing up with domestic violence has indeed left its mark and done its damage and if I thought that damage just fades away as we grow into adulthood, it doesn't and it didn't. I share this today because I hope it will make other parents stop and think about the damage of DV to your own children. Many times you hear people say they stayed in the relationship for the sake of the children. Children need above all else to feel safe, secure, nurtured and loved. Being with 1 stable parent is far better than being with 2 in a war zone. Even if you think that young children are not aware or you are shielding them from it, they are aware in their own ways and they cannot make sense of it. I will be forever thankful for my 'fortress' under the table but it would have been far far better to have not needed it in the first place.

You can find out more about me and my art and how it helps me on my website.

Kate Swift

This Tangled Web, A Constituted Charity.

www.thistangledweb.co.uk

Message from Eve – Thank you so much Kate for sharing this with us from your blog, your website is amazing and I encourage everyone to visit you. Kate gave her nomination to The Freedom Programme who then kindly passed it on to WAVE DV Centre. Eve x

CHAPTER FORTY TWO

I can't really remember the first time he hit me but I can remember it hurt like hell, the flat of his palm right across my face. At first it burned but then stung and no matter how much cold water I splashed on my bright red cheek the pain didn't seem to subside for ages.

The next morning I woke up and had a black eye and my cheekbone was swollen. I managed to cover it pretty well and went to work leaving him in bed asleep, he didn't come to bed until the early hours and so as usual I had tiptoed out of bed my clothes waiting for me in the spare room. I couldn't take a shower, it always woke him up and so every night I scrubbed myself clean making do with a quick wipe down with baby wipes in the morning (I couldn't even run the water in the kitchen, that woke him too and I never flushed the toilet although he was always made about that when I got home from work, I never could win.)

I knew that my days at work would numbered, he hated me leaving him alone in the house all day. I pleaded with him that we couldn't afford to put food on the table let alone the house if I gave up work but his relentless demands and almost constant physical digs were pulling me down, I had no fight left.

I gave up work for him in 2005 and it was only weeks later that it all ended.

From the moment I gave up work he knew he had me where he wanted me, his demands were extreme and he said I was his slave now. He would have me dress up in lingerie whilst doing the housework and liked to order me on all fours whilst

I picked the bits of fluff and crumbs up off the carpet by his feet. He didn't like the vacuum cleaner, said it was too noisy and made the pain in his head even worse, (he suffered a lot with pain in his head.) He wanted me to wear high heel shoes all day whilst doing the housework even though the pain in my back and legs was unbearable. The constant punches and kicks over the years had gradually damaged my lower spine and I urgently needed an operation but I knew I would be too vulnerable and totally at his mercy and so I refused the surgery.

Every day he would bark his orders and wouldn't even turn the TV over even though the remote was on his lap, he would shout me and tell me to turn it over whilst usually running his hands up and down the back of my legs until his fingers were inside my dry vagina. He liked to hurt me, he liked to watch my face as I grimaced in pain and so over time I learnt to adopt a passive look, trying not to flinch as he rammed his fingers in and out of me, spreading me as wide as he could. It would usually end with him sending me sprawling onto the floor with words like "you frigid slag, fuck off and get me a beer."

When he brought his buddies back one night from the bar I was curled up fast asleep in bed. They woke me with their rowdy voices and when the door was flung open and my husband appeared something told me I had to fight for my life.

What occurred next was the worst experience of my life, I wanted to die, I wish they had killed me that night. My husband ripped the bedclothes from my body and then ripped my night gown exposing my naked body to his friends who had gathered around the bed. I will never forget his words.

"Boys it's a fuck feast, time to get your dicks hard."

I won't tell you the rest, I can't I'm sorry but for the next two weeks I was kept as a sex slave, used at will. They were taking drugs and forced me to, I didn't know where I was, I wanted to die.

My husband left me, he just disappeared and thankfully his buddies went with him. I never reported this, I was too afraid. I am still married to him legally, I don't know where he is but I moved across the country to a completely different state. I have changed my name, my whole life to become free. I know he is out there somewhere but I'm no longer scared because I have a new life, a new man who loves me for me, my flaws and all.

Thank you for giving me my voice, it feels good. I would like my nomination to go to Rainn if possible.

A survivor!

Message from Eve – Wow! You are so strong. All the survivors/victims amaze me in this book, you are all so brave and I am in awe! Thank you so much for sharing your story. May your life continue to be happy and I have noted your nomination and will notify the charity. Thank you. Eve x

CHAPTER FORTY THREE

I'm not really sure my story warrants being in this book but after sharing it with Eve I guess she thinks it will fit and so I put my trust in her.

In 1984 I met the love of my life, my soulmate. We had four children together and were very happy, I was blessed. We had a lovely home, my husband was an engineer and so although we were always careful we never went without the nicer things. I was spoilt; my husband adored me and often splashed out and surprised me with lovely little gifts, tokens of his affection. I loved Bill very, very much and my family and home were very happy.

I miss Bill very much; he gave me the best years of my life. Never did he lift a finger in my direction and he hardly ever raised his voice, lets put it this way if my Bill raised his voice then you knew it was bloody serious and you had better get your arse in to gear pronto! Someone was in big trouble and with four children and an angry husband chaos was never too far away.

Bill never raised a hand to his children either; he abhorred violence and said that a stern voice was all that was needed. Our two boys and two girls were very well behaved and were quick to learn that disappointing one's parents was far worse than a slap on the backside. My youngest in particular really hated disappointing us and I was always the one to cave in when Bill and I were snuggled up in bed and discussing whatever problem had arose, he would laugh at me and hook his finger under my chin before looking me in the eyes. He said that's what he loved about me the most, my innocence and my motherly protective instincts.

Bill sadly passed away in 2006; we had 22 wonderful years together. For me that was it, I had loved and given everything to Bill, I had nothing left to give anyone else.

In 2010 I was at a friend's daughter's wedding when a gentleman approached me and asked me to dance. He was rather handsome and as we walked towards the bar after dancing he guided me gently, his hand on my elbow.

He seemed nice and so when I found out he was a friend of my friend's husband and a widow I thought nothing wrong in giving him my number.

He took me on a series of dates and wooed me slowly, he said he was afraid of getting hurt, his heart was still fragile but by early 2012 we were married. He would never replace my Bill, Ian knew that as I would never replace his wife but life was short and even though I didn't have very strong feelings for him he was a good egg and so I thought what the hell.

Within weeks I began to see flaws and begin to suspect that something was wrong, Ian was changing and it was quick. He was usually so attentive but lately he'd been disappearing for days on end blaming it all on work. He seemed stressed and so when he returned after being away for a whole week, I ordered some take away and opened a bottle of wine before plonking myself down on the sofa at the side of him. I took his hands in mine and looked him in the eye and asked him what was the matter, I could sense something, something wasn't right.

Ian began to cry, he literally broke down in front of me, I had never seen a man cry like that before. He was in trouble, he had gone into business with a friend and he'd basically ripped him off for over £80,000, Ian was at risk of loosing everything and I couldn't bear to see the wreck of a man who was sobbing into my lap. I was crying hard too, I hated to see him like this he was in so much pain. When I asked him why he kept disappearing he said he was working all the hours good sends, often not sleeping trying to make it work.

I couldn't stand seeing him like that and as the days passed he sunk further into depression, threatening to take his own life because he had messed up so badly, I was distraught and didn't know what to do and so I offered to help him, I was married to him so what was mine was his so to speak.

Alarm bells were going off in my head, I have to admit that and something in the back of my damn brain was screaming at me to stop what I was doing, it was wrong, how I wish I had listened.

The next day I went to the bank and withdrew all of my savings including the money left over from Bill's insurance policy, there was £85,000 in total. It took a couple of days to sort out but I transferred it into Ian's account without a bat of an eyelid, I trusted him he was my husband, he loved me.

Four days after the money left my account Ian disappeared and I never saw him again for two days. When he returned I was almost hysterical having had no reply from all the texts and voicemails I had left him, I thought he was in real trouble and someone was out to get him.

He sauntered through the front door a smug smile on his face, I was mad and demanded to know where he had been.

His fist smashed into my nose that quickly it's like a flash when I think of it now. The pain was immediate and the blood was gushing from my nose. I ended up having to have reconstructive surgery, the injuries were that bad.

I never reported my crime, I was scared no one would believe me and to be honest I feel stupid and very embarrassed; I trusted a con man, a thug.

I know I've lost my money but I don't care, I live on my own with my dog (guard dog!) I don't care. I'm happy and yes my life has been pretty shit but I only think of the good times with Bill. I am lucky I have loved, I have experienced true love and whenever I think of Bill I smile. If he was alive, well this wouldn't have happened anyway but he would have done more than punch Ian on the nose!

I haven't seen or heard from Ian since and I don't wish to.

Thank you for hearing my story and if you include it in the book thank you.

Jane

Message from Eve – Hi Jane I know it has taken a great deal of courage for you to share your story, I know how you have struggled but you are such a strong lady and I wish for you your Bill smiles every day. Your story has every right to be here too, your voice is as important as everyone else. Eve x

CHAPTER FORTY FOUR

Hi my name is Ann and I am a survivor of domestic violence.

I was married to Mark for just over ten years and at first we were happy until the kids came along.

He always said he wanted children, a football team he said but when our first baby was born he straight away hated her. Mark was used to having me to himself and so any time I spent with my baby was usually spoilt with him screaming and shouting abuse.

Every spare opportunity he had he wanted sex, he had a high sex drive but I was knackered, I got anaemia when I was pregnant and all I wanted to do was sleep. Mark did sod all in the house except make a mess and he always seemed to be either drinking or eating so if I wasn't looking after the baby or cleaning up his mess all I wanted to do was sleep, even half an hour would have been good but no Mark wanted sex, said I was neglecting him.

He was quick with his temper and even quicker with his fists and feet, he got a kick out of hearing me beg. Make up sex usually followed a beating; I was never in the mood for his kisses or false words.

A quick blow job usually did the trick but more often than not he liked me on all fours with my ass in the air so he could thrust in and out of me. He would spit on his fingers and wipe them around himself because I was dry and it hurt him putting himself inside me, it hurt him, it fucking killed me!

He would always moan and say I was useless and to be honest I felt useless. I didn't want sex anymore, I wasn't attracted to him and I was tired.

It wasn't long before I was pregnant again; my eldest had just turned 18 months when the little one was born. Mark didn't believe in birth control, he was catholic and said it was a sin to take it and prevent God's will. I wasn't so sure and I didn't know if my body would be able to stand another pregnancy.

It did but this time I got postnatal depression really bad, I hated myself, I hated him. I loved my babies but I often thought they would be better off without their mum. The abuse continued and got worse and I became ill, really ill both mentally and physically.

I tried to take my life a couple of times and ended up being sectioned, I hated the hospital at first and the nursing staff even more! They followed me all the time and never gave me any space or peace.

I know now that was for my own good. I opened up in hospital eventually and told them everything and now me and my children are living happily. It's been a long process, I've had to prove I am capable of looking after my kids but do you know something it was Mark that brought me down, Mark who made me ill, his abuse made me ill, not me, it wasn't my fault.

Victim blaming is wrong, very wrong and I hate it when I see stuff in the papers and on TV. No one asks to get hit; no one asks to be called names.

I will never let another man abuse me, I know the signs now and I hope that after reading the stories in this book you all recognise the signs too.

I wasn't sure about writing this story but it's made me feel stronger and I really hope it helps someone else.

I have new friends now and I am building my life back up. Me and my kids are doing fine, we are so happy and do loads of stuff together. Now I'm the best mum I can be, my kids are my world, I would die for them.

Thank you.

Message from Eve – A really moving story and one that shows you are a true survivor and a very strong woman. You were at rock bottom but you fought your way back up, I'm honoured you have shared your story. Thank you. Eve x

CHAPTER FORTY FIVE

Everyone thinks their childhood was "normal" I know I did until I grew up and looked back on it. When I was 16 my Mother entered the hospital several months before her 37th birthday, the same hospital that she passed away on May 20th 1984, I was a junior in High School and a typical teenager. I loved music, shopping, boys the typical teenager. The day my Mother died I can remember like it was yesterday. My Father was in the U.S. Navy and was away a lot of the time so my Mother was the integral part of our family. My Dad was not really ready to be a single parent of 3 teenaged girls and he did the best he could but we were no help. My older sister and I had after-school jobs at a local fast food restaurant and had made several friends from school that also worked there. I loved the job and I loved the atmosphere of all of us friends working together. That is where I met my "High-School Sweetheart". We were friends before we were a couple because we both had other partners but we all hung out together and worked together and went to school together. When I was 19 I got pregnant, had my daughter and got married, in that order. I was nowhere near ready to be a Mother but my Mother did it at 18, why couldn't I? So I married that "High-School Sweetheart" and six months after we were married was the first time he beat me. 14 years, 4 months, and two weeks into our marriage was the last time he beat me. After the first time he beat me I went to his Mother, my Mother-in-Law and told her. I didn't tell my Father because he would've wanted to beat him up or something. So his Mother looked straight at me and said words that resonated in my head for years after,

"You married him, You have to put up with him the way he is. What did you do to piss him off??" What did I do to piss him off, that is what my mantra was for a long time and as it turned out most everything I did pissed him off and if I didn't do something he found something. That's just "how he was".

When my daughter was born she was 3lbs 2ozs and 21 inches long, she was 2 1/2 months premature. They told me she seemed to be developing fine and that she would be a little behind but that she should catch up, well, at 9 months she still wasn't developing as I felt she should, she wasn't even doing any of the things that a 2 month old would do so at 11 months I had her checked by a team at a Children's Hospital in Connecticut and she was diagnosed with Severe Cerebral Palsy, Cortical blindness, and Epilepsy. A big diagnosis but as her Mother I didn't get upset, I didn't cry, I was relieved because we finally knew what was wrong with her and that now we knew what we had to do for her next. Well her Father was not so supportive, He questioned her paternity because there were no "retards" in his family and then he said words that should never come out of a Fathers mouth. He told me that he didn't, couldn't and probably wouldn't ever love her because she wasn't "normal". So I did everything for her alone, doctors' visits, alone, neurologists, alone, optometrist, alone, physical therapy, occupational therapy all done alone, unless I could talk one of my sister's into helping which they definitely did if at all possible. My daughter's Grandmother told me I should think about putting her away because they have "places" for kids like her. I refused every time it was brought up, she was MY daughter I could do it and I did, alone. Just an everyday activity like getting ready to go to school was a project because that entailed getting her up, bathed, dressed, fed, braces on, settled into her wheelchair, all for her 6:30am bus that came to take her to a school almost an hour away, I loved the school she went to and the staff there helped me more than I can say. When she was 13 she started having grand-mal seizures that would last sometimes 45 minutes long, talk about a scary thing, so she was admitted to a hospital to evaluate exactly how to control her out of control seizures, everything they did was not working. In the meantime, my own Father was diagnosed with Testicular Cancer and on June 7, 1997 he passed away.

I never worked a whole lot when I was married mostly because it was easier for me to take care of our daughter and he had no patience for her at all. I truly didn't like having to leave her alone with him for any reason. After I had my daughter I had two miscarriages and I was diagnosed with endometriosis, which I had a surgery for and 3 months after the surgery when our daughter was 8 years old, I got pregnant with our only other child, a son, my husband was elated at the thought of having a boy, and he was really good with my son, until I noticed he was mimicking his Father's behaviors at the age of 3, calling me a "Slut" or throwing things at me calling me a "Bitch" well that woke me up in a big way, I decided to leave. I went to live with my older sister in my Father's house. It was 4 bedrooms so we had room but it was a mess, I couldn't and wouldn't let my kids live in it, I didn't want to so I left the kids with their Father, I just couldn't let them live in the filth. There were bugs, food, garbage and you name it. My sister lasted 4 days living there with me around then she left after a huge argument about how I couldn't even have my kids there and she had a kid and she shouldn't have to live like that either. After my older sister moved out my younger sister moved back after finishing school in Boston. Her and I started finally getting the house in shape and then found out that the house was already in foreclosure with her just getting out of school and I just getting independent there was no way we could come up with the money to get the house out of foreclosure so we let it go. What a project that was and in the meantime my daughter's doctors were saying that it would be better if she stayed in a residential hospital/school until they got her medicine stabilized and working and she also had scoliosis and had to have an iron rod put in her spine, So needless to say with my daughters medical issues going on and my Father passing and all the time we were spending together, my husband and I decided to make our marriage work, to put our family back together. This is about the time I started seeing a "heart" whenever I was frustrated or upset or just needed reassurance. On a particularly hard emotional day before I moved back in with my husband I sat in my car and I asked to the sky, really speaking to my parents and I said I need to know if going back is the right thing or not, when I got out of my car there were hundreds of heart shaped leaves and I took that as a sign that, Yes, I was doing the right thing, So, we got a brand new house, brand new everything, brand new life. Only this time I had already had a year away from him, I did learn that I deserved to be treated with love and respect and I was prepared to call it quits if he started abusing me again. I told him I was no longer afraid to call the cops if I had to.

So we had some new rules to go with our new house. He was not to get drunk and he would not yell at me or call me names and he would not hit me. Writing those rules, it looks ridiculous that I had to barter for him NOT to hit me and I went back? Our first big fight in our new house was about our daughter, my then 4 year old son had mentioned how "Daddy dragged his sister to the potty by her feet" I was livid, HOW could he do that and HOW could I have left her there with him. A four year old kid just doesn't "think" something like that up, no imagination on a four year old includes abuse but he didn't hit me that time. Our second big fight was because while I was unpacking in our new house I kept finding nip bottles stashed here and there, he had NOT stopped drinking. That was one of the rules that he said he was NOT going to follow and there was nothing I could do but deal with it. He said he wouldn't quit for me or our kids, nothing was going to make him stop drinking. He didn't hit me that time either. That week is when I started to pack up some stuff of my own, stuff I knew he would ruin if I had left it there, the American Flag from my Father's casket, picture albums and stuff from my childhood, sentimental stuff to me and weapons for him to hurt me with. I packed it up and put it in my friend's basement storage area. I knew it would be safe there. Then I started calling the Battered Women's Shelters/Groups/Therapists, anyone who would listen to me so I could tell my story. They listened and I got scared with what they told me. NONE of the Shelters in Rhode Island where we lived were handicap accessible and I didn't know how long my daughter would be in the hospital, I wanted to make sure that when she got released, I would have the accommodations for her. I also found out that it would not cost me anything until I worked then they would charge a minimum fee but I didn't have to worry because I would be safe, and so would my son.

The weekend before I left was when we had our last big fight. It was on a Sunday which was Beer/Football day at our house. My husband's game that he HAD to watch was not being played on our system so he went to the local bar down the street because I refused to drive him, he had lost his license due to a drunk driving charge that he had for 12 years. I don't even remember falling asleep on the couch but I remember being woke up by him pulling up my t-shirt and groping me, telling me to get upstairs because he wanted sex. I told him I would be up in a minute because I wanted to grab a drink. Well, to him that meant I DIDN'T want to have sex and sent him into a tirade, pulling my hair, punching me in the head, then having me pinned to the floor with his hands around my neck, the thought actually went through my head that my son was going to find me dead and that thought terrified me, so I fought back, that is when he bite me on the thigh so hard that I truly thought he had taken a chunk out of it, then the next morning he couldn't remember anything that he had done, he apologized and even mocked me by saying "So now you are going to leave me right? If you take my son from me I will kill you, no matter what, if you take my son I will do it" he was sober and he was serious, I could just tell, he meant it. So that whole week, I think he knew that I was going to leave, he would take the car keys to work with him and I was no longer allowed to go anywhere alone with my son, who was already in Kindergarten at the time. I was in a panic and I didn't know what I was going to do. We did our normal Friday routine, Beer Store. Grocery Store, rent a movie, then back home. I had to go out for something we forgot and that's when my plan fell into place. Something told me to tell him the car broke down. I parked the car at an abandoned factory just down the road from our house, put the hood up, I then rubbed some engine grease all over my sweatshirt, left a note saying I would be back in the morning, in case the police wanted to tow it. Then I made the short but very, very long walk home. I was petrified that he would want to go to the car, but it was already dark and I had that as my advantage. So I got to the house took a deep breath and went in, so scared that he wasn't going to believe me. My fear was wiped out because he totally bought it, he called to secure a ride to work in the morning and all was "normal" we watched the movie "Big Daddy" but I couldn't tell you what is was about, my mind was racing the whole time.

The next morning, I got up made the coffee and got my son fed and my husband was off to work. I knew I didn't have all that much time because people my husband knew would be driving by, seeing the car, maybe seeing my son and I, so I rushed my son down there, we got the car and I went back the house to get what I could. I grabbed a basket full of clothes and a few favorite toys for my son and the eight dollars I had from change from groceries and we were gone. I drove to a payphone and called the Domestic Violence Hotline from the number I had memorized 1-800-799-SAFE (7233) and it is the same number in the U.S. now. I called and all of the shelters were full. I was petrified; if I went back he would know I tried to leave. They said that I could go to a homeless shelter but that my privacy would not be protected and there was a chance he could find out where I was. I got back in the car and wept like a baby, right in front of my son. He patted my leg and said "Don't worry Mommy, We can go to Aunt Missy's house" of course he was right, my younger sister had just moved into an apartment and my husband didn't know exactly where it was. I called her and I told her I had left my husband for good and that I couldn't and wouldn't go back. She said "Sure Come on over" I was relieved but also scared because I knew we could only stay the weekend, she lived in an all adult building and children weren't allowed. So we went over to her house and I wasn't even in the door before I started crying again, this was not going how it was supposed to and I didn't know what I was going to do next. So at my sister's house I hit the phone. I called and finally secured a room for my son and I at a shelter that was 70 miles away from where we were so I could feel safe that he wouldn't find me. I had to wait till Monday but I was ok with that because I knew I was on my way to being free.

Besides my Mother in Law, I had never actually told anyone of the abuse, mostly because it would cause more beatings but also because I was embarrassed because I let him treat me the way he did. After talking to the Shelter worker though, I felt better, I wasn't "crazy" I wasn't "stupid" and I definitely could get on with my life without my husband. I didn't tell my son exactly why we were leaving, he was only four. I told him that Mommy and Daddy just couldn't live together. That we were going to start a brand-new life in a new place. I also told him that once we got settled, he could see his Dad whenever he wanted, that Daddy was mean to me but that he loved his son, which was true so the following Monday, we took the ride to Middletown, Ct. to a shelter with a fitting name "New Horizons" was a perfect way of describing the way I was feeling. The town in Rhode Island where we lived in was small, a one red-light town, where everyone knew everyone or they were related, so when my son and I went up over a hill and saw the "city" we were about to call home, I think we were both overwhelmed with the size of it. I told my son, "Here we go, going to start a brand new life" and he looked at me and said "Mommy, is it okay that I am a little scared?" I told him of course it was that even I was nervous but that it was going to be good for us. So I called the shelter when we arrived and the worker came to escort us to the shelter. When we pulled up to it I thought we were at the offices for it, but going in, I saw I was wrong, it WAS the shelter. I had an image of green walls and cots and a bunch of women sitting around wondering how they got there. But it was a home; it had six separate bedrooms, two bathrooms, two living rooms, and the kitchen. It was nothing as I expected but better. We got assigned a room and introduced to the other two women and their kids who were now my "roommates" sitting on the bed in our new room, my son playing cars on the floor, I took a deep breath, and then another, and then another. I was relaxing, I had gotten away, I was free and alive, and we were going to be fine.

I called my daughter's workers and let them know where I was and that I may not be up to see her for a while, I pleaded with them to not let my husband know where we were, and they never did. Three very long months later, I finally got to go see her, unfortunately her father was there visiting also, with his Mother and his brother. My daughter had just had her back surgery and I was holding her at the time she was 14 years old and almost a big as me. My husband came barging in the community area that we were sitting in yelling "Where the fuck is MY son" there were approximately 6 other handicapped students there and the horror on everyone's faces told the story of the atmosphere, he was yelling all kinds of obscenities at me and my son ran and hid behind the rocking chair I was sitting in with my daughter. I told my husband that it wasn't the place to do this and that he needed to calm down, fast. I told my son he could come out and say Hi to his father and he did. When my husband picked him up, I looked over and saw my Mother in Law holding the door. I told the girl from the shelter who had come with me NOT to let him leave with my son, I got my daughter situated into her wheelchair and went over to get my son out of my husband's arms, he said "NO, You are not getting him" and with that my son reached for me and I pushed my husband with all I had, I got my son out of his arms and he slapped me square in the face, right there in front of everyone. My Mother in Law said to him "I told you not to hit her, now the cops are going to come" at that point he didn't care, he smacked me again called me some choice words and then they left, before the cops came. This is when I knew that I was in trouble, I was not safe anymore, they had put my new address on the police report, he was going to know where I was. The next day the director from the shelter took me right over to the courthouse and we got a temporary restraining order and I felt a little better, not much but a little.

My son and I stayed in the shelter for a total of 6 months, usually they only allow the women to stay 3 months but with my situation being from out of state, not really having any family to rely on, they let us stay longer until I could find suitable housing for us. I had just gotten a job at a little cafe in town and I was so embarrassed that I had to give them a copy of the restraining order, to protect them too if he found out where I was working, they were totally supportive and understanding, I couldn't have dreamed up better bosses to have at that time in my life. Middletown had all day kindergarten, which was a godsend for this newly single mother, I could work when my son was at school, my bosses were so accommodating too, if my son was sick or had a day off, if I couldn't find a sitter, they would let me bring him to work with me, which he loved. So with a restraining order in my pocket I walked my son to school, walked to work and all the time I was looking behind me wondering when he would find me. Then the court day came to make the restraining order permanent, a court date that he HAD to show up to, I was scared to have to see him again. So with my lawyer, the director of the shelter, a worker from the shelter, and a friend of mine, we all went to court. He came with his mother, no lawyer, just his mother. When I saw him, he gave me the most evil eyes I have ever seen in my life. Then it was our turn, the judge called us and the lawyer, the Shelter Director and I all stood up, my husband and his mother also stood up. The judge asked my mother in law if she was the lawyer and she said "No, I am his Mother" he then told her this didn't concern her and to take a seat. FINALLY, someone told her our marriage didn't include her, I giggled on the inside. So, we reached an agreement where he could have our son every other weekend. I told the court that I didn't wish to keep my son away from his father but that I didn't want him drinking around our son either, my husband signed the agreement and we all left, I was elated. I really wanted to skip out of there, I was getting my independence back, but what I didn't realize at the time is that I was getting myself back too.

So every other weekend, I got someone to come with me and I brought my son to see his Father. In the meantime, I got my first apartment of my own. It wasn't in the best neighborhood, but it was mine. I felt such a sense of freedom and independence that I didn't even know I was missing. My whole life up to that point was a series of lies lies to cover up, lies to hide the truth of what was going on, and lies about how I really felt. But now I had nothing to hide, everyone who knew me knew why I was in Middletown, I hid nothing and it was so freeing. Everything I needed for my apartment was donated by a family in the next town over, I was to not know their names but they helped out with so much for me. They donated everything from living room furniture, kitchen stuff, beds, dishes, towels, you name it, I had it because of them and I was so grateful and wanted to thank them in person, but that wasn't allowed. I got settled in and I loved every aspect of my own place. Then at Christmas time a guy showed up with four huge bags of stuff for my son for Christmas, he told my son that Santa was busy so he asked him to deliver it, I had recognized him as one of the men who helped with my furniture and asked if I could have his name so I could at the very least have my son write a Thank-You note, he refused saying only, "Santa sent me" with a big smile on his face. That Christmas routine went on for the next six years, even when I moved across town to get my son in a better neighborhood they called his school to see if I would give them permission to get our new address, they brought stuff there too, it was many years after that, I finally tried to tell my son who it was doing this, at this time he was 11, but he didn't believe it, he just KNEW the guy was sent by Santa. I appreciated those people so much and I can never tell them.

So with a visitation order in effect and weekend visits going pretty good, I decided it was time to file for divorce but my husband had other ideas, he got the papers and promptly scribbled notes here and there on them, he told me he wouldn't sign them if I put the reason why I left was because of abuse, he was worried it would affect him on a professional level if anyone ever saw that. Needless to say the judge wouldn't even hear the case. He said to go back to the drawing board and figure it out. So after I saved up another fee to file for divorce I filed again, this time my husband sent them back all signed in the wrong places, on the back, front and the sides of the document, it looked like a 3 year old got a hold of it and the judge again refused to hear my case. At that point, I had given up, I didn't feel married anymore, I couldn't afford it, so I decided to wait some more time till he was ready. I just didn't want to go through all of the same thing again. So I went on with my life, had a few dates nothing special but I was getting me back and I loved it. I loved the sense of independence I was having, and I thrived in it. Around this same time I picked up an old hobby of mine that I love, writing. I wrote an essay about inner strength, I wrote about how I left my husband and I won 1oo dollars! I was chosen by the Director of the Shelter to do some speaking on their behalf, I spoke about my experience and the aftermath and I loved that also. I even spoke at a meeting to get the shelter moved because it was too accessible to the abusers being downtown where it was. And they got it! I wasn't ever a public speaker and for me to do that was a feat in itself. I just wanted to get my story out there, to let women know they COULD get away, safe. I know that if I had just left him and went to a friend's or relative's house it wouldn't have been as it ended up, he would have definitely killed me, I know that in my heart. Then came a day when I had to go by myself to drop my son off, something I never liked to do alone, that was when my husband decided that he was going to give it one last try, he pinned me up against the car, kissed me told me he wanted his family back and that he was thinking of moving to Virginia. I told him there was no chance of a reconciliation and that he should take his lessons learned, move down to Virginia and start all over, like I did in Middletown. He was not happy, but I got in my car and drove away. My son was 8 at the time and that was the last time he saw his Father.

Around Thanksgiving time is my son's birthday, I called my husband to find out about any plans he had for celebrating, but was told by his roommate that he had moved to Virginia but no one had a number or an address. So I let it go and finally he called my son, he told him yes, he had moved but that it wouldn't affect their relationship, that he would still see him for holidays and maybe in the summer. None of that came true, there were promises of visits that never took place, Birthday/Christmas gifts that were never sent and after a while my son caught on and just gave up. I felt so bad because here was a kid, who wanted so much to be a part of his Father's life only to be let down time and time again and my husband wasn't the one that had to deal with our sons disappointment, I was. I had to try to explain why he didn't call when he said he was going to, I had to explain why he wasn't going to visit even though his Father said he would, I had to do that part and it just about KILLED me. I tried to make his life as "normal" as possible but I know he carries that disappointment even to this day but he carries it in his heart. On one of the rare occasions that his Father called, he wanted to talk to me, so I explained to him that our son was 11 now, old enough to call, write, email or whatever he had to do to stay in touch with his Father but that I would not FORCE him to do it. Their relationship was between them, it had nothing to do with me. I never stood in the way of my son seeing his Father. He was not abusive to him, he was abusive to me. I did not want my son to ever accuse me of keeping him from his Father, I didn't want to be the kind of Mother that was bitter and cruel keeping my son from him out of spite because that always ends up being bad for the kids. He would end up being angry at me for it. I also didn't have a parade of men going through my house either, I was conscious that whoever I brought into my life I brought into my sons life as well and I was being picky about it. I dated a few men but my son only met very few. If it wasn't looking like a solid bond, I was not going to let my son bond either, kids get attached to people and get heartbroken when they leave, I never wanted to do that to my son, and I didn't.

We went on with our lives, and out of the blue, my sister in law called me. I was a little surprised since I hadn't talked to her in many, many years. I called her back and she told me that my husband was wrestling around with some friends, drunk of course, and they dropped him on his neck, he was paralyzed and he was going to need more surgeries. I was in shock and it all came flooding back, this was Karma at its best, he didn't want or love his handicapped daughter, now here he was, handicapped. She told me that I needed to file for divorce so that she got to have power of attorney to get medical services for him, since legally I was his "next of kin" she couldn't do it until we got divorced and she sent me the money to file. I couldn't have been happier. I felt no compassion for this man and I was happy he got to see what my daughter went through. So we waited the allotted six months and then on Jan 2, 2007; almost 8 years after I left him I finally got my divorce, the last hold he had on me was gone, I worked at the courthouse cafe, so everyone there knew I was going for my divorce and they were all happy for me too, I got flowers, cake, balloons, everyone was just so happy for me but not as happy as I was. With him being paralyzed I felt I could finally move back to my hometown, with no threat of him coming back, or stalking me, or anything.

So I spent 10 years in Middletown, and I loved it a lot, except I was away from my hometown and I was understandably homesick. When my lease was almost up, I started the process of moving back. I secured a job at a big Indian Casino and found a suitable apartment to live in; my son was 14 by now and a freshman in High School. I figured that since he had been going through the same school system for 9 years, it would be easier to start in a new one as a freshmen because everyone is new their first year of High School. I had some reservations because I was changing his whole life around and I didn't do anything without first discussing it with him. Luckily, his best friend from Middletown, moved a year later to his Grandmothers, which just so happened to be in our new town, so at least now he had his best friend. Moving back to my hometown area was a lot more emotional than I had thought it would be, first thing I did was to go by my Father's house, the people that were living there fixed it up a bit but the yard was full of old junk cars and looked horrible but they still had my Mothers lilac bushes intact which I was so glad for. It took me awhile to go back to the town where my now ex-husband and I lived, where a majority of the abuse took place but every time I go to see my daughter, even to this day, when I pass the exit, I get knots in my stomach, and I get nervous and have trouble breathing, all effects from the abuse. I got over it on the outside a long time ago but, my subconscious won't let it go. I have night sweats if he is in my dreams, even if he doesn't do anything to me in my dream, I wake up shaking and sometimes crying, the therapist that I worked with at the shelter said that will probably never go away. It is something I have to live with until my subconscious lets it go.

Now I had another fresh start in my mist, my son had a new school, I had a new job, was making new friends and my life was finally getting to where I wanted it to be. I finally put the finishing touches on the book I wrote about my abuse "Eight Dollars and a basketful of Clothes" and am now waiting for a publisher to pick it up. I am doing all the things I want to and I have no one to hold me back. My ex-husband still has limited contact with our son but I think that is my son's doing, mostly because he feels that when he moved to Virginia his Father basically forgot about him, I try to encourage him to at least try to have some sort of relationship with his Father but I think my son is too hurt to let go of it now, maybe when he gets older he will try harder but at this point he has no contact with him unless it is on Facebook and even that is scarce. It's a sad fact because my son has such a big heart and would easily forgive my ex-husband but there is no effort, and I think that is where my son's anger with his Father comes in.

When I moved back to my hometown area, I was still single, not really looking for anyone in particular. I had gone out with a few guys, but the ones who asked me out were all the young ones. Or they lied and said they didn't have a girlfriend/wife. I was not having much luck so I just decided to give up. I knew the signs of a potentially abusive man and although I never saw it in any of the men I went out with, there were a few with some question marks. I vowed to never let anyone treat me with anything but love and respect. I had loads of friends but I was lonely, I didn't know it then but I was. All of my friends were attached so I was frequently the 3rd wheel. My best friend and I decided to go to a concert at the Indian Casino where I worked to see a favorite 80's band of mine, she didn't really like them but she went with me so I didn't have to go alone. We got seated at a table where 3 men were already sitting, the guy straight across from me just kept staring at me and I just knew he was going to ask me out. Sure enough he asked my friend if I was single and she said "Yes" even though she KNEW I didn't like to be set up. He waited till the show was over and came up to us, he asked for my number so that we may get together for coffee or whatever, I was apprehensive to say the least, I told him I would find him on Facebook and contact him that way. It was four days later I got in touch with him with the encouragement from my friend. We got together for coffee and ended up talking for two hours. He had the most heartbreaking story to tell, just a short month and a half before he met me his only child passed away at the age of 18. She went to visit a friend she hadn't seen in a while and it's still under investigation but they truly believe that one guy that was at the same house drugged her drink with methadone. He had a difficult ex-wife, to say the least, and his daughter had finally come to live with him, they were in the process of repairing their relationship when she passed. Then he added that his on/off girlfriend of two years left him for his best friend that he had since he was six years old just a week before his daughter passed. It was the most heartbreaking thing I had ever heard and I was sure this guy was not into having any kind of new relationship at all but he asked me to go to Jamestown, R.I. a place I had been to many, many times before with my ex-husband, of course I was reluctant but there was just something about this guy I liked. So I finally had a date, with an honest man who even though his heart was broken in many pieces, he was open and I liked that.

The day when he came to pick me up is when I knew he was going to be a special person, he asked if he could meet my son but I explained that I would like to get to know him better and he understood. He brought me a bouquet of lilies, which I loved because I despise roses, which means he was listening when we were talking at coffee. Then I got into his car and looked up, he had a heart-shaped necklace hanging from his rear-view mirror, my sign, I looked at it, looked at him, looked at it again and said to myself "Give this guy a chance." So we were off to Jamestown which is a coastal tourist town, I absolutely love the ocean, and so does he. We both had so much in common and I couldn't believe that I had finally found someone just for me. He was compassionate, big-hearted, and handsome. He was accepting of BOTH of my kids and his Family was great too! On New Year's Eve 2012 he proposed to me. I always swore that I would never ever never ever get married again, but I said "YES" because this man is my soul mate. He would rather die than to say or do anything to hurt me. I know what real love is now, because of him. If I can reach one woman and make her realize if she is in an abusive relationship to get out, then I will feel good. "Love doesn't hurt" is a saying I wrote on a wall at the Battered Women's shelter and they are true words

"Love doesn't hurt" and there are men out there that love without hitting, talk without hurting and treat women with respect not as a possession. I am an internally happy person now, I know I am a good person, and not what my ex-husband said I was, it took me a long time and I still struggle sometimes with self-esteem issues and I still have nightmares, but I am happy and no man can ever take that from me again, I won't allow it to happen.

Message from Eve – WOW! You are one brave lady and how I smiled when I read your happy ending. Please tell your future husband thank you from me, from #OneVoice, there are men out there that don't hit and hurt but love and cherish. You have travelled so far and I know you will go on to help many. Much respect and deep admiration your way. Your friend Eve x

CHAPTER FORTY SIX

I am not really sure how to start my story or how it will really help and I know I don't have to be embarrassed because I'm a man who has suffered from domestic violence.

I met my wife in 1992, she was beautiful and all the local guys wanted to be seen with her, she was really popular and could have been a model.

I used to watch her whilst I served the other customers laughing with her friends; she was really cute and would twirl her hair around her finger whilst looking over at me.

One Saturday night she came in with her boyfriend, he was a thug and it wasn't long before they started to argue and he slapped her hard across the face, I was shocked. I'd been brought up that to hit a woman was wrong and my mum and dad had made sure that I knew how to respect the female sex. When he jumped up and grabbed her hair I knew I had to do something and although I was shitting myself I shouted as I walked over asking him to let her go. He punched me in the face knocking me out but when I woke up she was there, holding my hand.

It wasn't long before we were going out, I couldn't believe my luck, Lucy was gorgeous!

I was young and in Uni, she had a job as a typist and her own little flat, she asked me to move in after 5 months, I did.

Things were really good for the first few months but slowly her temper and her true side began to show, she wasn't cute or sweet she could be down right evil at times. Lucy would hit me with anything she could lay her hands on and her words were like venom. I knew I wasn't the hottest looking guy and she could do better, I knew I was lucky but did she have to tell me so much!

I ended up in A and E quite a few times with quite a few stab wounds where she had belted me with her stilettos. I've got a scar under my eye where she punched me and her ring cut me, the engagement ring that she demanded I buy and then took my credit card and went shopping for it herself! The wedding was much the same, I had no say, it was Lucy's day and so I smiled for the camera and went along with everything she wanted.

We went for our honeymoon to Barbados, Lucy wanted to go there and on the 3rd night I was ill with my stomach and she wanted to go out and party and so she went and left me alone in the hotel. Lucy didn't come back until 4pm the next day; I was so worried and had even been to the police to report her missing. I was really angry when she just strolled into the room, her hair a mess and make up all smudged around her eyes. She said she'd made some new friends and had been to an all nighter, sniffed coke and basically got pissed. I forgave her; she was safe, I was just happy she was alive. I wasn't keen that she had taken drugs but she always called me a prude whenever I voiced my concerns, she liked to sniff coke most weekends and then was in a bad mood for the rest of the week but as soon as she snorted her magic white powder she was happy again. I wasn't.

Lucy didn't need an excuse to be abusive and thought it was funny when I cowered to shield myself from her assaults. Not once did I ever lay a finger on her. I wanted too, I felt like doing, I wanted to try and restrain her many a time but it just wasn't in me.

Our marriage lasted five years, we never had kids but we did have a dog and Lucy had 15 affairs that I know of. The night when she disappeared in Barbados was a lie, well part of a lie she had gone to a party and sniffed coke all night but she had also took part in an orgy.

I got many STD's from her, I think the doctor at the clinic wanted to give me shares I was there that often. I tried to wear condoms but she wouldn't let me, "I can't feel your small cock as it is" she would say.

The end came when she left me for someone else, I didn't care.

It's taken me a long time to even be able to look in the mirror and very slowly I'm learning with my counsellor that I'm a good person and worthy of love. I was brought up never to raise my hand to a woman and I never have and I now know that Lucy took advantage of that.

I've date a couple of women since and even confided in one after the 7th date that I had been a victim, she laughed and didn't believe me, thought I was covering up and that I was the abuser. I'm not a weakling, I'm 6ft 3 and medium build, I like to work out and look after myself, I'm not your average looking victim!

I just want to say to all the women out there – men can be victims too and I would never doubt a woman so please don't doubt us.

I hope I can find somebody one day who will love me for who I am not try to change me and mould me into something they want.

Thank you for giving me this chance to help raise awareness that men too can be victims of domestic violence and abuse.

Message from Eve – Thank you so, so much for sharing your story and I hope it raises the awareness it needs. As I have said before not all men hit and especially not all big men hit! I am positive you are going to find your special one, GO YOU! Eve x

CHAPTER FORTY SEVEN

Michael was the love of my life and we dated for almost 3 years before he got down on one knee and asked me to marry him, I was so happy and began to plan our wedding straight away. We never got married. Three months later he was coming home from work on his motorbike and was involved in an accident with four other cars, he was pronounced dead at the scene.

I'm still not over Michael's death and I think about him every day, when I go to bed at night I see his face and he is always in my dreams, even my nightmares. He must be turning in his grave, he must be so angry.

I got married 12 months ago to someone who I thought I could trust but as soon as we returned from our honeymoon the violence and abuse began. I was his wife now, his property and I had to do as my told. He knew all about Michael I had nothing to hide and he had even sat on my bed with me and looked through a memory book I had made. My memory book no longer exists Jason burnt it and made me watch as it went up in flames. Every card Michael had ever bought me was either ripped up or destroyed in someway. I tried not to cry in front of him, tried not to show how much it hurt. Jason hated tears, said they were a sign of weakness and so I tried to hold it all inside.

He saved some of the cards for his hobby, his smoke, cutting them up into strips he would roll them for the end of his joint. I liked it when he smoked marijuana, he was chilled out and never violent, it gave me a break and sometimes he was even really nice to me. I wished he would smoke it all of the time because he slept so well at night too.

The physical violence wasn't too bad it was the words, the cruel words that even today I still have trouble with. I don't like the word stupid, I'm not stupid and I hate the word idiot, I'm not an idiot either. I'm waiting for him to agree to a divorce but he is being awkward, I can wait I have to.

I've moved in with my mum and dad again, I know I should get a place of my own at my age but I just can't afford it. I see him hiding sometimes, watching me and it scares me but it's so difficult to prove, I've got to catch him or have a witness because without them it's just my word against his and he always manages to come up with an alibi. He's been warned under the Harassment Act but he takes no notice, he's not daft! Part of me just wishes he would find someone new because then he would leave me alone but then the other part, the victim wouldn't wish his abusive behaviour on anyone!

I don't know if he will get me, I follow the safety rules and I try to be as vigilant as I can but I shouldn't have to live like this, it's no life!

Message from Eve – Stalking is terrifying and I hope he is caught in the act very soon. You have been very brave to come forward and share your story and I know you do so wishing to raise awareness. Thank you, stay safe. Eve x

CHAPTER FORTY EIGHT

Dear Tom

YOU ARE A PIG!

I have decided to write you this letter because I need answers but I doubt you will answer you are too much of a coward. I might not even send it yet I don't know. I don't know a lot of stuff really because you fucked with my head; you messed with my mind and played your games, YOU BASTARD!

What did I ever do wrong? Can you honestly look me in the eye and tell me I deserved it? I know I didn't fucking deserve it, I know I did nothing wrong I don't even know why I'm asking you. I'm done writing you this letter.

I need to vent, I need to have my voice heard and so when I came across Eve Thomas on Twitter I thought hey, I need to talk to her, she's cool. I watched for a while and had a look at her website and then thought what the hell, what do I have to lose after all? No one needs to know it's me, its says that on Eve's website, yes I wanted to be heard.

She's a really nice lady and asked me if I was in a safe place both physically and mentally to do this, yep I sure was. Ok I'm still pissed off, you would be if you went through what I did and yeh, yeh, yeh I know there are woman and men far worse off than me that have been through far worse than me. I've never been hit, he threatened to but he never went through with it. Ok, he pinned me up against the wall a few times but that's because I was trying to smack him one after he had to point out for the 100th time that day how fat I was getting. I wasn't fat I was pregnant!

Before you say it no I wasn't violent, well I had never been before I met Tom, he used to have me so frustrated and hurt that I would lash out, I'm ashamed of that, it isn't me.

Our daughter was born and you loved her from the minute you saw her, you forgot about me well except to continue your emotional abuse. Now I was used goods, ready for the knackers yard and you made of a point of telling me that our daughter was the new girl in your life and I was no longer needed.

You never let me be a mother, you never let me try. Every time she cried you were there, that's if you weren't holding her, she was your possession and I couldn't get a look in.

He controlled everything, our daughter, the finances, the house. I didn't have a say on anything. If something needed buying for the house Tom picked it right down to the curtains and cushions and knick knacks. I wasn't allowed to be a woman and it hurt a lot.

Tom didn't like me wearing make up either or having my hair down and he thought that hairdresser were a waste of money and so everyday I just scrapped it back, stuck on my joggers and got on with whatever I was allowed to do. I wasn't even allowed to cook for my family, he did it all.

Tom called me lazy all the time but whenever I tried to help he would throw me one of his looks, scold me like a child and then turn his back on me. We didn't have sex, he didn't touch me, he was never kind but he never hit me so I thought I wasn't abused that somehow I was failing.

I was lonely and very unhappy and wanted to run away but even though my daughter wouldn't even come sit on my lap I couldn't leave her, she was still my baby.

Tom eventually had a heart attack and died, our daughter was 14 and we didn't know one another, we are working on our relationship and it's difficult but I am sure we will get there. She constantly tells me I am useless, not her dad and how it should have been me that died, I agreed at first but now I don't.

I've woken up! After following Eve on twitter and reading her tweets I sought help and for the first time in a very long time I don't feel useless. My daughter is having therapy too and I hope one day she will love me as I love her. She is very much like her father but there is hope.

My head is messed up, I'm still very angry but as I have wrote my story I have felt calmness come over me. This was supposed to be a letter that I was going to leave on Tom's grave but I've decided not to, he's just not worth it.

Message from Eve – As I read your story I could also feel the "calmness" come over your words. I'm so in awe of you. I hope that your relationship with your daughter continues to grow in strength day by day. Be happy. Eve x

CHAPTER FORTY NINE

I was born in 1944 and in 1966 I was married to Graham. We had a family quickly and it was shortly after our second daughter was born that the affairs started. Graham worked on the doors and would not come home until the early hours, usually drunk, usually violent.

He would storm through the house waking me and the girls up, demanding food and a hot drink. It was bedlam, my babies would be crying, which just made him shout even more but I couldn't attend to them he wanted feeding.

My life continued that way for many years and the violence just got worse and worse. I remember one Sunday going to church, the girls loved going to Sunday School. When I arrived home, it was late afternoon there had been a function that I had helped out with, I walked up my stairs and into our bedroom to find my husband in bed with another woman. I didn't know what to do. What was my reaction supposed to be? Yes I could have screamed and shouted but that would have just got me a beating, it was better to stay quiet. The bitch smirked at me, I will never forget her face, his arm was casually around her shoulder. She was pretty but I could tell she was a tramp, a slut.

It was never mentioned again, I had quickly left the room, got the girls coats back on and walked back out of the door, I sat on that park bench watching the girls play like a zombie, I smiled and laughed when they did but I was taking nothing in. Things were bad very bad and I didn't know what to do.

Graham controlled everything, the finances, the house, everything. I even had to ask for money for food every week and he would reluctantly hand it over usually with a slap as well for my cheek at asking for money to feed my family.

I didn't argue, I never answered back I just carried on. He threatened to leave me a few times and my heart would skip a beat but then he would say he was taking my babies and so I knew I just had to put up with it, make the best I could out of the hand I had been dealt. Life was crap!

My husband beat me for the last time when our youngest daughter was 12, I managed to escape fleeing to a neighbour who was embarrassed as he had heard the abuse but never intervened and here was me hammering on his door, blood pouring from my face and asking for help.

Graham was arrested, he didn't go to prison, domestic violence was nothing back then. I got remarried a few years later but that didn't work out either, he wasn't violent but he was an alcoholic and I'd stood it once there was no way I was going through that again!

I'm now almost 70 and I am still bitter. My girls are grown and have babies and families of their own and even though I met a nice man a few years ago and we cohabit very peacefully I'm still bitter. I don't want to be but I just can't help it. I see Graham on special occasions like weddings and christenings and we are polite to one another but I will never, ever forget the feel of his fist on my face, I think I will take that to my grave.

Message from Eve – When I received your story I knew I had to include it in this book because I feel it conveys an important message. Years ago domestic violence wasn't recognised, it was a domestic and that was that and so victims have never received justice. Stay happy. Eve x

CHAPTER FIFTY

feel alone. I get on websites offering the chance to make new friends and all I get are a bunch of people after sex. I just want someone to talk to, someone who I can laugh with, cry with, watch a movie with, or even just chat with online – without the thought of sex entering the picture. I just want a friend. A real friend – someone who I can be myself around. I don't even know who that is, but I'll never find out if my whole life is spent trying to defend myself or compete with other people for my kids' love. I shouldn't feel like there is a competition because I know my kids love me more than anyone else in the world but I just don't feel like I'm being the mom they need. They need someone who can be around them without being sad about the things she can't do. There are so many things that I can do, but all I can think of when they are around is what I can't do. Barney is on lesson 17 in quizzing, and I haven't gone through one lesson with him. He has moved on to his second home reader and I haven't gone over any of the stories with him. I don't know what my kids are learning in school. They are gone for a few days and I lock myself up in my room all alone and barely even speak to anyone else in the house. Even when they are home the only time I come out of my room is to complain about something that somebody did or was doing, usually something that doesn't even matter in the whole scheme of things but I turn it into the biggest deal I can. It's like I want to be miserable. I feel like I don't deserve to be happy. I killed somebody. I killed somebody who really did love me. He loved me. He loved the boys. We all loved him. I don't know what would have happened that night if I hadn't gotten the gun out. Would I have survived the night? Would I have had the guts to leave if I did survive? Would he have – I don't know. I can't change it. I can only try to get through it. I need to be a good mom to Barney and Noah. They are such good boys. They have been through as much hell as I have and they are caught in the middle of this whole thing, only they didn't do anything to deserve it. They have always been good kids. They need me. They need me to be there for them. They need me to care for them and talk to them and listen to them and play with them and just love them. They need me to let them live without getting mad about every little thing that happens in our lives. I need to pray more. I need to go to church. I need to put God first. I just don't know how. I need to take care of myself and lose weight and clean my room and help mom around the house and stop taking so many meds and stop being so depressed. I need help. The way things are right now, I think everybody would be better off if I just went away to prison for a long time. I am keeping so many people from leading happy, productive lives. I don't want to be a cry baby to anyone. I don't want to be so depressed. It does hurt. It hurts me. It hurts my kids. It hurts my mom and her family. I need to start living again and quit sitting in this room doing nothing but watching TV all the time. I seem to be doing okay at typing again. I don't know if I could do it all day or just a few hours a day or maybe just a few hours a week, but I can type a lot easier than I could before my surgeries. I've got to start getting out there and quit being so self-conscious. I'm fat, but I don't have to be. It will take time to lose the weight. It took years to gain it all, and it takes longer to lose it than to gain it. I'll never get where I want to be, though, until I start getting out in the world. Pay off my debts, save some money for my kids and my futures. Get out and live. Find love. Real love. I don't know if I could ever love anyone the way I loved Brian. He was the guy for me. He was my one true love. And I killed him. He died over a remote. It almost seems ironic that the remote he couldn't find turned out to be the one that he threw at Noah. I had reached for that gun so many times in the past, but I had never actually felt the need to use it. That night, though, I did. People tell me about all the things I should have thought about before I shot him. They don't seem to realize that I was too scared to think about anything. All I knew was that he had hurt me in the past without even meaning to. He had threatened me on the way to the ER, telling me he was sorry for hurting me while at the same time telling me that it was my own fault, threatening my children if I were to tell anyone what really happened. He had scared Noah so much that night that he could hardly breathe and I had to leave him in his bed while he was so scared just to keep Brian from coming in there and hurting him for taking away the attention that Brian thought should be on him. He was always so jealous of the boys because I wanted to spend time with them. I missed them when they weren't with me. I didn't miss Brian. He never gave me a chance to miss him. He was always there, on the phone, on the computer, in person. I was so excited about him going to Atlanta. I thought I would finally get a chance to spend some quality time with my kids. Even from another state he managed to get in the way of any attention the boys might have gotten. I wanted so bad for him to be gone. I wanted him out of our lives, but I didn't want him dead. I wanted him singing his music and playing his guitar and having a girlfriend so that his attention was focused on something other than me. It would have been better for him to be too busy to spend time with the boys than for him to continue not being busy and still not spending time with them. He kept me from spending time with them as well. All they had was each other. I wanted to stay in our house. I wanted to be rich, to have enough money that my kids could have everything they wanted without having to use credit cards. I wanted to be able to take them places and not worry about how much it cost. I wanted to stay home with them and eat frozen pizza on a blanket on the floor while we watched a show and not have to spend most of that time on the phone with Brian. I wanted to love him the way I used to. He wanted that, too. I don't know how much of who I loved was really him and how much was the high him. I want to believe that he really was that guy I fell in love with. I've always wanted that. I miss him.

I haven't been to church since the Christmas program where the kids sang "Here Comes Santa Claus" with a big blow up Santa. In Santa We Trust on the candy bar was too far, but I never had a problem with Santa before Brian. It's the only thing he ever tried to teach our kids that I am okay holding on to but it's tearing me and my family apart. It's keeping me from God. I want my life to be lived the way God wants me to live it, not lying in my bed all the time watching TV because I'm afraid to have a conversation with anybody. I do want my own place to live, but I'm not ready for that. God put us here for a reason. I will never lose weight watching movies in bed. I will never feel better health wise until I lose some weight. I want to feel better. I want to play with my kids. I want to go out without being embarrassed by my appearance. I am who God made me to be and I need to accept that and go from there. I need to quit letting Satan control me and my actions.

I can't figure out what happened the night Brian died, and it's making me crazy. When did I fire the shot that went through the walls? Why was the shell casing back with the first two shots? What position was he in when the bullets entered his back? I remember him getting up, and I remember being afraid that he was going to grab me and my gun and shoot me. I remember being afraid that he would kill us all if I didn't get the kids out. I remember Noah being so scared and crying so hard that he could barely breathe, and I had to leave him in the room alone to go be with Brian just to keep him from coming into their bedroom because I knew that if he had to come in there to get me, he would have killed Noah. He would have regretted it immediately and killed himself, but I truly believe that he would have killed Barney and I first. He was such a sad soul. And I realize now that I knew nothing about him, the real Brian. The guy I fell in love with was a fake. He was happy. He was Brian on meth. Sometimes I wish that I had just "gotten over it" and not been so obsessed with keeping meth out of the house. He was happier when he was doing it and not trying to hide it from me. What I don't understand, though, is why he didn't just go ahead and do it the way he wanted to. He did everything else the way he wanted to do it. Maybe he just used me not wanting it in the house as an excuse to do large amounts in one sitting. I don't know enough about it to know what a large amount was or what it cost but I do know he came home from the club high at least twice in the last few months of his life. He acted like he didn't know he was high. Was that real? Did he really not remember doing it or did he just not want to hurt me anymore than he already had? I know a lot of his anger was because of his feelings about himself. He couldn't stand to look at Noah because it reminded him that he was high on crack when Noah was born. He couldn't stand to look at Barney because it reminded him of all the times he screamed at Barney and smoked meth in front of him. He couldn't stand to look at me because he had hurt me so badly so many times. He seemed to have a really, honestly good, heart. He just couldn't get past his past. I don't miss him anymore, most of the time. It has been over a year. If he was still alive and we were just divorced, I wouldn't miss him at all. I miss his music and the look in his eyes when he would sing. Not that look he always had at the club that made it so obvious he didn't want to be there but that look he had when he would sing at church. I only ever heard him sing at New Life but it brought tears to my eyes every time. I'm crying now just thinking about it. He wanted to be a better person, but he let pride get it in the way every time. Pride and a lack of self-confidence had him trapped in a place he didn't want to be. All he had to do was humble himself and follow God. He wanted to follow God. I say that and then I think, is that true? I never realized how little I knew about who he really was until now. He was always high on something or mad that he couldn't find anything to get high on. His brain was messed up from so many years of drug abuse. Or maybe it was messed up already and nobody knew it. I don't know. I'll never know.

When I found out my aunt was missing my first thought was that her abusive ex husband had come back to Arkansas. I was wrong, thank God and she is home safe now. It was nothing more than a car stalling in the middle of nowhere shortly after her cell phone was lost, giving her no way to simply call for help. I'm journeying into the past, a past before I met Brian, I do that often, my mind wanders a lot.

I know it may sound off-the-wall to some to think her ex had come back into town but not to someone who has been in that situation. I've had an abusive ex who found me and tried to kill me. I was saved by the only man who was brave enough to come to my apartment. He was there the night my ex was hiding in the closet with a knife. People always talk about how easy it is to leave someone who abuses you, but how can they know if they have never been in that situation? With my first husband, I had no children. It was only my life I was risking by leaving and leaving wasn't easy. I couldn't go to my mom's. He knew where she lived. He said he would kill her and I both if I went there. I had to move away from everybody I knew. My mom did help me get a new car, and I left with nothing more than what I could fit into my car. He found me at work, though, before I was able to find a different job. He watched from across the parking lot to see which car was mine. He said he had found my lease for the apartment I had moved to in my car. When he was in my car, I don't know, it was probably while I was at work. He came to my apartment many times. He raped me repeatedly. I called the police but he was always out the next day if they had found him at all.

With Brian, things were different. He was the man who saved my life so many years ago. He was my knight in shining armour.

I met Brian in September 1999, I was 24 but very naive. The first time I got drunk was at Henry McNuff's Country at the Halloween party 1999. That was when Brian and I started seeing each other. He just happened to be with me when my first husband followed through on his threat to kill me for leaving. We had not been divorced long, and I had no plans to get into any kind of serious relationship for a very long time. Brian saved me that night and helped me move into his parents' house. He was my hero. We knew each other less than a year when we got married. I just knew he would never hurt me. We split up twice in the first three years. I was devastated the first time. I drank a lot and cried myself to sleep almost every night. Brian wouldn't speak to me in public, and when we were alone he said everything he could think of to hurt me. Yet he still called every night to say he loved me. I was so confused.

We got back together after about six months. I took care of him when he broke his back that fall. By the end of the year we were fighting again. He wouldn't let me go with him to the club for New Year's Eve. He came home the next morning with one of the bartenders. He took her into our bedroom and locked the door. I moved out the next week. This time I got a second job rather than drinking and crying. We spent more time together during the separation than we had when we were living together. We even filled out divorce papers but never filed them. After about three months, he and his mom got into it really bad. I was at the house with him. She tried to set my car on fire because he wouldn't let her in the house. She was very drunk. That was when we decided to move to Nashville and start over. A year and a half later, we had our first child.

Things started to get bad after that. It's like he was jealous of any attention I gave our son instead of him. When we moved back to Arkansas, he started back on meth. I found out later that he had been doing crack in Nashville. I don't know why I'm telling you all this. I keep going over our entire marriage in my head...over and over...trying to figure out what could have been done differently. It wasn't as though we were happy one day then he started hitting me the next. It started small. A slap in the back of the head was nothing compared to my first husband. Before I even realized what was happening I was following his orders, keeping my opinions to myself, being the best little servant girl I could, and still getting hit. I did everything I could to please him but nothing was ever good enough. Everything I did was to make him happy but you can't make someone else happy. After two trips to the emergency room - one concussion and one broken wrist I gave up trying to make him happy and started just trying to keep him from getting angry. And now here I am.

My kids have no father but they are thriving.

Most of the time, I wish I wasn't me. I wish I could erase the last 20 years and still have my children, just as they are. I'm prepared for whatever happens at my trial. As long as my boys are safe I will be okay. I've been raped, beaten, gun to my head, bones broken. I've been called every name imaginable. I've been held captive. I've gone months, sometimes years without seeing my family. I can't think of anything that could happen in prison that is worse than what I've already been through.

I wasn't thinking clearly when I shot Brian. I was in panic mode, more scared than I had ever been. All I wanted was to get my kids somewhere safe, somewhere away from him. I did run once, before Noah was born. I managed to get Barney to the car and get away but I had no idea where to go. I knew he would catch up to us before we got to the freeway. I saw lights at Mark's house and we went there.

I got into so much trouble for running and for involving his family that I never did either one again, until October 14 2011. I wanted to run. I tried to run, but I knew he wouldn't just let us go. I thought that if I had the gun he would back off. He didn't. That night was only the second time I had ever pulled the trigger. I had the gun for 2 1/2 years. We always talked about going to gun safety classes or going somewhere to learn how to shoot but we never did. We talked about doing a lot of stuff that we never did. There were so many times that I thought things were better. Sometimes they were better, sometimes they weren't. I've spent 17 months going over and over that night doing the "what if" thing. The only thing I can come up with that I truly believe is that if I hadn't shot him he would have killed me. He would have then killed the kids just to keep his parents from raising them. Then he would have killed himself.

He was ready to kill John Wilkinson, Mary, and Martin and that was fairly early in the night. I did manage to calm him down a few times but it never lasted and he wouldn't let me out of his sight. Not until the end when he just completely lost control and started destroying everything and screaming that he was going to kill me. That's when I got the gun and starting trying to empty the chamber. And now, here we are.

My kids come home Sunday afternoon - Barney is saying things that I have heard Mary say so many times but have never heard Barney say. Suddenly, after 4 nights in a row at their house, he doesn't want to go to church or do Bible study and saying that his daddy never did anything bad to us because the only reason he locked them in a room and yelled a lot and hit me all the time and broke my wrist etc etc was because he was sad and mad and it wasn't wrong for him to do that stuff. And Noah wants to punch Granny in the head because she doesn't like black people and its okay to hit people. Ugh!

Sorry - I haven't slept much at all this week. Barney came home very "argumentative" about stuff like bedtime and church and just things that he's never argued about before, at least not any more than any other kid. He told me that his daddy didn't do anything wrong because the only reason he locked them in their room all the time and hit me all the time was because I made him sad and mad and that makes it okay. Noah came home talking about wanting to punch Granny in the face because she doesn't like black people, and the only reason he hasn't is because only daddies get to punch mommies.

I know that isn't anything Mary has put into their heads, at least not intentionally but I've spent all week trying to figure out how to bring it up to her without upsetting her. I'm trying so hard to bring peace back to the family.

He would sleep until noon and get angry if I didn't have a hot breakfast ready when he woke up. I would offer him what the boys and I had left from our breakfast and lunch but he didn't want it. By that time, he would be upset because it was too late in the day for breakfast and I should make him lunch.

If I said I had a headache, at any time of day he would get mad because he thought I was already working on my excuse not to have sex that night. We did it 3 or 4 times a week, even with 2 kids but he didn't think that was enough. He would also get mad and say I ruined the mood if I wanted to lock the bedroom door before I got naked. I just didn't want the kids walking in on us. For a long time I had to put a sock in the door frame just to get it to lock. I wanted to fix it but he said he would. After almost a year, I finally gave up waiting for him to fix it and did it myself. I got in trouble for that too because I was supposed to let him do it. Most of the door frame was still in the floor behind the armoire when he died.

He always told me that fibromyalgia is just an excuse women use to be lazy. When he would pinch my elbow or my knees trying to tickle me he would take it as a personal attack if I accidentally let an "Ouch" slip out or a reflex pull away from the pain. He thought I just didn't want him to touch me and that always made him angry.

I don't know what to write about. There are so many things to say…

Brian never trusted me because his mom had a 20 year affair and used him as her "alibi" so that she could go see her boyfriend without her husband finding out. I paid all the bills but he always demanded statements from everything. He kept the cash in a lockbox and hid the key. Every once in a while he would give me a $20 bill as my spending money.

I was treated more as a servant than a wife. He would walk through the kitchen and sit down then tell me he was thirsty. He never asked me to get him a drink; I was just expected to do it.

Even at supper I made one meal for the family (which consisted of me, him and 2 kids) one meal for him because he rarely ever ate what I cooked the first time (although when I asked what he was in the mood for he would say "just make something!") and another meal for the kids (which I didn't let him know about.) He got very angry if the kids didn't eat what I made, which never made sense because he didn't either. I made his drink and took it to him…made his plate and took it to him…refilled his drink and took it to him…then I was able to get the boys something to eat. He always ate in his recliner so he could watch TV. The boys would sit at the dining room table. On the rare occasion that I actually had time to sit down to eat, I would sit with them.

He always wanted me in the room with him, whatever room he was in but the boys had to stay in their own rooms. He would get angry if they took my attention away from him. He worked from home but wouldn't "go to" work unless I went with him. So I would sit and watch him work while the kids were locked in their playroom. I would watch them on the baby monitor but I had to keep the sound turned all the way down so that he couldn't hear it. He constantly called me fat-ass, bitch, whore and lazy. He made me wear clothes that were so loose I had to constantly pull on my pants to keep them up. Anything smaller than that was too tight for someone as fat and ugly as me.

He was convinced I was faking my disability just to get out of cleaning the house. He always complained that it wasn't clean enough. He wanted everything right there where he could reach it without having to lean or stretch his arm out or anything but he couldn't stand for anything to be on the surface of a table. He couldn't stand for anything to be in a corner either. He would knock stuff on the floor just to get the counters clean. He figured that if I couldn't walk through the house without stepping on it then I would clean it up.

I had to get his towels for him when he took a shower. Then he would dry off and walk through the bedroom to sit in his recliner in the living room. I was expected to get him some clothes. He would get angry if he had to actually tell me to get him clothes. Most of the time I wouldn't get the right clothes the first time…just like the meals.

He wanted three meals a day – and a sandwich was not a meal, it was a snack. A meal was made up of meat and potatoes and rice (usually) and maybe another vegetable.

I couldn't disagree with him on anything without him accusing me of trying to start a fight. We did not talk about anything. He talked and I agreed or we fought.

He called me stupid a lot and never believed anything I told him about things (like the fuzzy stuff in the air vents in the car meaning that the in-cabin air filter needed to be replaced). I told him about that once because I remembered from the first time it had happened. He said I was wrong. When I tried to remind him that it had happened before he accused me of calling him stupid and hit me on the back of the head. A few weeks later he told me that somebody had told him that it meant the in-cabin air filter needed replaced. He believed them.

He was always hitting me on the back of the head.

When he went to Atlanta for computer certification boot camp he called me over 200 times in 10 days. That doesn't count the many, many text messages or the video chats every night. There was one video chat where he got mad because he could hear the kids playing in the background. That is the one that turned into a regular chat session. My lawyer has a transcript of that chat session.

My mom wasn't allowed at our house and I was not allowed to go to her house. We didn't see her for a little over a year before Brian died.

When I was working, he would call me several times every day. Anytime he called me, I had to answer or he would get very angry. If it rang too many times before I answered, he demanded to know why it took so long. When he would text me, I had to text back immediately. There were several times when he would accuse me of forwarding my office phone to my cell phone because he was hearing so many people in the background and was convinced that he was hearing sex noises. I would call him back from the phone in my cubicle so that he could see where I was but he would then accuse me of somehow programming my cell phone to show up as my office phone number.

I couldn't sit through meetings in my boss's office without him calling and like I said I had to answer or he would continue to call. He accused me of sleeping with my boss because I had one on one meetings with him.

I couldn't eat lunch with my mom without him calling 4 or 5 times during the 30 minutes we had for lunch. I couldn't eat lunch with anyone else period.

When he would call for me across the house if I didn't answer immediately he would accuse me of ignoring him. He would never believe that I just didn't hear him. He would call Barney out of his room so that Barney could get his remote for him. He had a sticker with a dot in the middle to mark his remote. Nobody was allowed to use his remote.

He was always going through my computer, my phone, my nightstand, my dresser, my purse, anything he could find to go through. He would try email addresses with my name in them (even though they were not my email addresses) and threaten me and usually end up hitting me if I didn't tell him the password. Since they were not my email addresses I didn't know the passwords. He was convinced they were my secret email addresses that I used to keep in touch with my imaginary boyfriend. He never seemed to comprehend that I'm not the only person on the internet named Christine Baxter or even Christine Lisa Baxter.

I was never able to keep a journal or type up a document like this because he would have found it. I couldn't let someone else use my phone to call anyone because he never would believe that I wasn't the one who dialed the number. Anytime I got a call from someone who dialed the wrong number he called me a liar and a whore.

He would put a pillow over my face so that I couldn't breathe, "just playing around". On multiple occasions though he said "I swear one of these days I'm gonna smother you in your sleep." For many years I was unable to go to sleep until after he was asleep just because I was afraid of what he would do to me. I think that is where my anxiety about having anything close to my face came from.

He called me stupid a lot yet had me doing his school work for most of his online college classes.

He "tried" to kill himself several times. He would take a lot of pills – mostly my pills that he would hide from me. Sometimes he would pretend to take a lot of pills just to see if I would try to save him. The one time I saw him put the pills in his pocket and didn't try to save him he got very angry and hit me several times.

He only let me take my meds when I had a doctor's appointment just in case they did a urine test on me.

He would put his gun to his head and beg me to pull the trigger for him. Marcus Middleton talked a little about that incident in his statement to the police.

He used to point his gun at me threatening to shoot me if I didn't tell him the name of my boyfriend, which I didn't have.

He once ran me and Noah out of the house with his gun because Noah, a 6 month old at the time was crying. When I was going to classes to try and become a teacher Barney would stay home with Brian but I had to take Noah to my dad's or my sister's. He could barely stand to be around Noah, possibly because he was high on crack when Noah was born. It was a scheduled C-section and we got into a fight over who was going to drive me to the hospital because he didn't want to get out of bed that early. After my 2nd night in the hospital the nurses asked if I was ready to go home, I said yes but then Brian said "If you're going home then I'm going to get a hotel room for the night so I can get some rest." I cried and told the nurses I needed an extra night at the hospital.

When he had a doc appointment we all four went. He didn't trust us without him and he didn't trust himself without us.

When we lived in Texas he wouldn't let me tell them about my unemployment from Arkansas because it would have affected our Medicaid and Food Stamps.

He refused to help with any house cleaning because "That's the woman's job." It didn't matter if I was working forty hours a week while he sat at home doing nothing all day.

He made me get his weed pipe ready or use a rolling machine to roll him a joint knowing how badly I wanted the stuff out of our lives. He would smoke in the house no matter where the kids were. He even smoked weed in the car with the kids.

If anything ever made him angry while he was driving, which happened pretty often, he would drive really fast and crazy and scary not caring that our children were in the backseat.

Barney and I ran out once when he was high on meth and threatening us both with a gun. When he went to the bathroom we took off to his brother's house. I was afraid to leave the property because he would have caught up to us.

He drank a lot.

I can't think as clearly as I used to.

When he would scream at me, I couldn't think at all.

When he was upset about some customer service issue he was calling about he would give me the phone and say "Take care of it!" Then he would yell and cuss so much in the background that I couldn't hear the person on the phone and they couldn't hear me which only made it more difficult to try and work out a solution. I would end up crying. They would keep apologizing and asking if they could do anything to help but they couldn't do what he was demanding because it was so outrageous.

He blamed me for his weight gain – said it was because I didn't cook healthy meals – but he wouldn't eat them when I did. Instead he had me cook something else or go to McDonald's.

I had to take the kids with me everywhere I went, including the OB/GYN. They would sit behind the curtain while I was naked on the table with my feet in the stirrups.

I wasn't allowed to go anywhere but doctor visits or grocery shopping.

He called constantly anytime I was not with him.

I hid my son's bedwetting from him because we would have both gotten in trouble if he had known.

He threatened to "never come home" when he did go somewhere alone but threatened to either take the kids from me or kill me and the kids and whoever we were staying with if I left him.

He wouldn't let me wear make-up but got mad that I didn't make myself pretty for him.

I had to get his permission before I could make plans for anything, even just lunch with my mom but I always ended up having to cancel the plans at the last minute.

He would apologize for hitting me but tell me it was my fault. He said I should know better than to get in his face but it was always him coming to where I was standing/sitting.

Fall 2010 – he was screaming at the kids (then ages 5 and 2) to "Get this fucking room clean or I'll bash your fucking head in!" I stepped just inside the living room and I asked him to calm down – said I would help them when I finished cooking – reminded him how young they were. He came to where I was – said "What did you say to me?" I repeated "Just calm down. They're little." He pushed me. I hit my head on the corner of the piano...broke a laundry basket on the way down, which slowed my fall. After a few minutes, I had a huge knot on my head and couldn't open my mouth. He finally took me to the emergency room. I only had a concussion but it was three months before I could open my mouth wide enough to eat a sandwich again. The part of my head that was injured is the muscle that controls jaw movement.

Jan 2011 – It started the same way as the fall 2010 incident except that I stayed in the kitchen. I wanted to get his attention off the kids but I didn't dare move from where I was standing. That's where I was when he pushed me. We had tile floors. I hit pretty hard, broke my wrist bone into two completely separate pieces. On the way to the hospital he said that I should have known better than to get in his face like that and that if he got even one hint that the police were coming for him, I would never see my kids again.

After my surgery to repair my wrist he told me that the doc said I had brittle bones. He made me ask the doc for a bone density test. Doc refused because there was no need for it. I had never broken a bone before or since.

His attitude at home was dependent on whether or not he and his mom were getting along. They didn't get along often.

He made me do sexual things I did not want to do.

He threw things a lot.

He would get on to me if I didn't do something the way he wanted it done.

He thought everything that everyone did was based on how it would affect him – basically thought the whole world was out to get him.

If someone cut him off in traffic, he got mad because they did it on purpose. If I said "Maybe they just didn't see you" then I was taking their side against him.

I'm currently awaiting trial for 1st degree murder; this is my story a jumbled mess like my life.

*names have been changed for legal reasons.

Message from Eve – When this lady first made contact on Facebook I was pleased that she was reaching out and wanted to share her story. I sent her a quick email to check that she was in a safe place to write, her reply left me stunned. "Yes I am safe from my abuser, I killed him." Since that initial message I have found out more about this very courageous but lost young woman and I wanted to help her and her two young boys. She was arrested 7 months after she shot her husband, yes that's correct 7 months and despite being honest from the very start with the police and authorities they still arrested and charged her with 1st degree murder. She is due to go on trial in July of this year and has had thousands to pay in legal fees as she tries to defend herself and her boys, her parents are in debt as they struggled to put up bonds and so #OneVoice has decided that this chapter's share will be donated and go towards this brave ladies legal fees. Once these fees have been covered the money will then go to charity, a charity that will be her decision.

I have purposely left this chapter, this very poignant story until last as it shows the extremes that can happen in a relationship dominated by domestic violence/abuse. This poor woman is now facing not only a trial but a prison sentence because she genuinely was in fear of loosing not only her own life but those of her boys. What would you do in you found yourself in that situation? I know I have questioned myself over and over again and had I been just that little bit stronger back in the day and had a gun to hand would I, could I have shot my husband, the father of my children dead? When he was yelling abuse at my girls and throwing his threats around to set us all on fire could I have killed him? For years I lied, for 21 years I lived a lie now I'm free, I'm me and so I am going to answer this question that I have posed honestly.............YES! I could easily have shot him dead! Would I have regretted it? YES because at the end of the day, no matter what he did or who he hurt he is still a human being, the father of my children and although my girls don't want anything to do with him, he's hurt us all too much, I some how and don't ask my why wish that one day he finds peace but he can only do that if he admits he is an abuser and that he will never do.

I want to thank you for sharing your story with me, with the world; you have helped to show what can happen when domestic violence/abuse goes too far. You are now on trial for your husband's murder and I'm going to be honest, my husband wants to thank his lucky stars that he's alive and breathing because had I been in your situation I probably would have done exactly the same! I wish you all the luck in the world and want you to know that I stand very firmly by your side and offer you my full support. Survivors not victims! #OneVoice!

THE END

I have shed a lot of tears whilst getting this book ready but I have also made some wonderful new buddies, women and men the same as I, SURVIVORS!

I've shared their pain and their joys but most of all I have applauded each and every one of them because they are all so brave, so inspiring and I am in awe of each and every one of you.

Some are beginning the journey, some have travelled far but all have the passion, the need to want to help others. We all hope that this book of true stories, our lives, travels far and whilst on it's very own journey raises awareness and puts domestic violence and abuse firmly in the spotlight.

For many, many years voices have been silenced it is now time for change. A #OneVoice voice will NEVER be silenced!

As the very first #OneVoice book goes to be published I had an idea – There are many victims and survivors out there who are in pain and need a friend, someone to talk to, to share with, to off load. #OneVoiceBuddies is a brand new #OneVoice project where all victims and survivors are welcome, a place to make new friends, a warm and safe environment where you can chat and as you gain one another's trust hopefully pair up and provide the support that is needed with the gentle guidance of our team of tweeters.

#OneVoiceBuddies are not professionals but we are professional victims and survivors who just want to be there for another in need.

You can find #OneVoiceBuddies on Twitter by following @OneVoiceBuddies or on Facebook. Come join us, the coolest befriending support service EVER! The links to #OneVoiceBuddies can be found on my website as well as a heap of information.

For now I shall leave you but wanted to say thank you again for purchasing this book and if you recognise any of the signs contained within its pages please reach out and always remember YOU ARE NOT ALONE!

Until next time...................

Stay safe.

Survivors not victims!

#OneVoice breaking the silence; NEVER SILENCED!

Eve x

www.evethomas.co.uk

Printed in Great Britain
by Amazon.co.uk, Ltd.,
Marston Gate.